THE MIRACLE, THE WITNESSES AND ME

HOW 26 MINUTES AND THE POWER OF COMMUNITY PRAYER CHANGED EVERYTHING

Charlma J. Quarles

Charlma J. Quarles Copyright © 2023

EMPOWER ME BOOKS, INC.
A Subsidiary of Empower Me Enterprises, Inc.

No part of this book may be reproduced, stored in a retrieval system, or transmitted in any form or by electronic, mechanical, photocopying, recording, scanning, or otherwise, without the publisher's prior written permission.

Scriptures marked KJV are taken from the KING JAMES VERSION (KJV): KING JAMES VERSION, public domain. They are used with permission.

Scripture quotations marked (NLT) are taken from the *Holy Bible*, New Living Translation, copyright ©1996, 2004, 2015 by Tyndale House Foundation. Used by permission of Tyndale House Publishers, Carol Stream, Illinois 60188. All rights reserved.

Scripture taken from the HOLY BIBLE, NEW INTERNATIONAL VERSION®. Copyright © 1973, 1978, 1984 Biblica. Used by permission of Zondervan. All rights reserved.

Scripture quotations are taken from the Amplified® Bible (AMP), Copyright © 2015 by The Lockman Foundation. Used with permission.

ISBN: 978-1954418219
Printed in the United States of America

DEDICATION

This book is dedicated to anyone who has ever heard or thought that "prayer does not work"; "there is no hope"; "he/she is not going to make it"; "they probably will not survive the night"; "call your friends and family so they can say goodbye"; "there is nothing more we can do"; or "he/she will never be the same".

ACKNOWLEDGMENTS

Thank you to the "Witnesses": all of you. A special thank you to Dr. Clifton Clarke who declared to me that my testimony had to be shared widely and, to do so, I needed to write a book. His words took root, my spirit agreed, and here we are.

Thank you to Temaki and Patrice, who helped shift the atmosphere of the ICU, bringing captive the words that were elevated against the knowledge of God! I Corinthians 5:10

Thank you to Khaliah who reminded me that context is everything; to Phillipa for hearing my voice; and to Sonya for seeing what I saw.

FOREWORD

By Samuel Alan Burroughs, Sr.

We first met Charlma on a Sunday morning in the spring of 2002 at Petworth Community Center in Washington, DC. We were in the embryonic stages of a church plant called, The Outpouring Ministries. Our weekly gatherings at Petworth intersected with Charlma's journey on that day. She would later say that the sign above the door, the music, and the Holy Spirit, drew her into the building. My wife Merilyn and I were unaware that this was the beginning of one of the most important and wonderful relationships of our lives.

Not long after, Charlma joined the Outpouring. She later would be a part of the staff of Elders and fully expressed the virtues and values of what the young church was striving to become. A faith community must value God's word, prayer, worship, service, faith and the flexibility to follow the leading of the Holy Spirit. Charlma became one of the pillars of our church. She is a friend to everyone she meets.

Our tight knit faith community was rocked to its core the day after Thanksgiving 2015. We were devastated by the sudden loss of our beloved worship leader, and friend. The loss of such a beautiful soul still weighs heavily on our hearts. "It was unimaginable that almost 3 years to the day we would experience an event with Charlma that would change us all." I recall telling my wife, "I'm really starting to hate Thanksgiving."

When news arrived that Charlma fell deathly ill, the shock and pain caused an explosion of faith and aggressive prayer that was fueled by the Holy Ghost. Throughout the following pages, Charlma will share the details of her ordeal and the response of those in relationship with her. The impact of the weeks and months following Charlma's illness was unexpected. The growth of our collective faith and maturing of our prayer life through her pain is nothing but miraculous. It would be narcissistic to assert that her suffering was for our growth. What occurred was not about us. Yet, God decided to pull some of us close. He allowed us a front row seat to witness the wonder of his power. Despite the dark days and grave circumstances, the Lord imbued us with supernatural assurance.

We are the witnesses who have been forever changed by God's amazing grace.

Samuel Alan Burroughs, Sr.
Pastor, Emmanuel Temple Pentecostal Church
Boston, MA
Resides: Bowie, MD

TABLE OF CONTENTS
There are different ways to read this book.

DEDICATION

ACKNOWLEDGMENTS

FOREWORD

Section I: FIRST THINGS FIRST..........................13

        My Testimony...Our Story
        The Witnesses: Major part of book
        Prayer: The power that fueled
        "MIRACLE"- An Overused Word

Section II: WALES 23

        From Wales to the Emergency Room
        Red Herring – What happened before
        November 21st.

Section III: Strategic Positioning........................29

        Strategic Positioning- Emergency Room
        Strategic Positioning- The Hotel Pickup & Urgent Care
        Strategic Positioning- The First Call for Prayer
        Strategic Positioning- Medical Personnel
        Strategic Positioning- The Security Officer and his Wife

Section IV: THE MIRACLE| PRAYER- POWERFUL.........43
                 PART OF THE PROCESS

        Branches going everywhere
        The ICU became a place for Praise and
        Prayer around my bed

Let it flow like the river Jordan—Specific Prayers
When prayers are answered, some people are perplexed

Section V: THE MIRACLE: WITNESSES........................69

    The Witnesses
    The Nos and the Knows
    Chosen to Represent: The two cousins
    God will finish the work: Outpouring Worship & Life Center
    Warrior, Guardian, and Comforter
    The Girls
    Up from Alabama
    You were in there
    A miracle, witnessing a miracle
    Soldiers
    They saw for themselves
    What will happen to Charlma?
    Let the children come
    Were Angels There?
    She got down on her knees
    Where was our patient on the chart
    Book of Esther; perhaps I was there for a purpose

Section VI: THE MIRACLE: Ripple Effect..................150

    The Ripple Effect: More than they expected
    The Ripple Effect: New boldness came forth

The Ripple Effect: "Confidence was released in me that night"

The Ripple Effect: What is going on here?

Section VII: Me; throughout the process...............168

You don't belong here

I was not fighting for my life: God was in control

Dreams

Sua Sponte

My rehabilitation

She spoke in a different language

You will dance again; and so, it was

You are a miracle; dead and now alive

Clothed and in my right mind

God makes all things new

Ninety-nine percent mortality

How would I know?

His expectations were higher

No Broken Bones; Not One

Circling back

Waiting for the other shoe to drop

It happens at some of the craziest times

Power in the process

Section VIII: Second breath of life hike; celebrating anniversaries.................................227

Reflection: Not Routine

Poem: Jesus is still a healer

BOOK REVIEWS

AUTHOR BIO

⟫⟫ HOW TO READ THIS BOOK ⟪⟪

My hope is that all who pick up this book will read it in its entirety, because I believe as the events changed my life, perhaps some portion of it can impact the readers as well. However, reading it from beginning to end is unnecessary because you can read the chapters out of sequence and still get something from them. There are eight sections of the book with individual chapters under all but two of those sections.

Section I: First Things First contains general information that may be helpful when reading the book. Some of the information in this section takes the place of the Prologue in most books. Under the other sections, most of the chapters stand on their own focusing on various aspects of my testimony, which means that it is not necessary to read the preceding chapter for you to understand the chapter you are reading. Good examples of this are the Sections "The Miracle: The Witnesses" and "Me Throughout the Process." Under these Sections, you can pick chapters out of sequence to read, and they should still make sense. All the chapters are short in length, some of them are just a few paragraphs. Again, how you read it is up to you.

SECTION I
FIRST THINGS FIRST

MY TESTIMONY AND THE WITNESSES; OUR STORY

This book tells of events that started when I went to the Emergency Room the day before Thanksgiving 2018, continued during my time in ICU, later in my hospital room, after my release in January 2019 and beyond. When the doctors determined that there was no more that they could do for me as I laid on life support, people prayed, and God miraculously brought me back from the grips of death to a state I had not previously experienced. A seemingly hopeless event turned into an inspiring and unforgettable journey. While this story is my testimony, you will see that it is also the testimony of many others as well; it is our story.

THE WITNESSES: MAJOR PART OF THIS BOOK

Although this book is based, in part, on my first-hand experiences, text messages, e-mails and medical notes, an incredibly sizable portion of this writing comes from the experiences of several people connected to me. They told me about their experiences; what they saw, heard, thought, and felt. These people include family, friends, associates, medical personnel, and work colleagues. Some have dual roles: friends who are like family or work colleagues who are also friends. I call these people in their varied roles *"Witnesses."* They were around me before, during and after my hospitalization. Many of them heard what was being said about me when they visited the ICU. Others were in the right place at the right time and their presence was not coincidental.

Most of the stories from the witnesses were told without any prompting from me. Some people began talking about a week after I was transferred from ICU to my private, restricted hospital room[1]. The doctors had initially

---

[1] I say restricted because there were age restrictions for my visitors and, at some point, all my visitors had to wear face masks and disposable gowns.

discouraged my friends and family from mentioning anything to me about what I had been through if I did not remember it. Since the doctors were not sure of what was the root cause of what happened to me, they did not want to cause me any stress just in case stress would somehow result in a relapse. So, for the first few days of being in my hospital room, everyone was quiet and extremely cautious around me asking only how I was feeling. But then, as though it was just too much to contain, a few people started telling me things. They could not keep what they had seen, heard, and experienced to themselves anymore. Others, however, did not start sharing things until months and even years after I left the hospital. A year or so after I left the hospital, I asked a few people what they remembered or what they experienced during the period of me being hospitalized, but for the most part, the witnesses shared their feelings and experiences on their own. Sometimes, I would be engaged in a conversation with someone and in a 'by the way' fashion, they would mention something that occurred with me or with them during that period. Other times, people felt compelled to share an experience with me while we were engaged in some activity that no one thought I'd be able to do again when I was in my worse condition in the hospital. Although people were present at different times during my journey, there were common themes that everyone shared concerning me even if they talked about them differently. There are other people who have never mentioned anything to me or said extraordinarily little and I respect their internal processing of the events.

Without what I learned from the witnesses; portions of this book would not be possible. For example, when I was in a coma unaware of my surroundings, it was those around me who shed light on that period. So, in large part, this book is as much about others as it is about me. These witnesses are the leading characters in this story. Although I sometimes speak in generalities when referring to a witness calling them "friend," "colleague," "co-worker," or just "someone," this book is unique in that I have decided to mention names…a lot of names. Some names I mention several times and other names I mention only once. Please do not let all the names distract you; you don't need to keep up with who is who like you would in a novel that was weaving a complex plot.

PRAYER, THE POWER THAT FUELED

What does prayer have to do with this story? Some may ask "Can't we just hear about your story without talking about prayer?" Well... quite simply, the answer is No. It would not be possible to avoid this subject because prayer was connected to every part of my journey. To be clear though, this book is not on the forensics of prayer: what prayer is or is not, when to pray, or the specific words to say. I share about focused, community prayer that took place and the miracles that occurred in my life. Texting some people asking them to pray was one of the first things I did when I sat in the triage area of the ICU waiting for my vitals to be taken. Regardless of the processes and procedures that would be administered by the medical staff, I knew that the first order of business had to be prayer. Prayer was also the means through which other people were able to participate in the miracle that God was performing. Prayer was interwoven in everything.

'MIRACLE'
AN OVERUSED WORD

> Miracle: "An extraordinary event manifesting divine intervention in human affairs."[2]

How many of us have been part of conversations where someone described an event as a 'miracle'? Probably most of us have. If the event being discussed was, as the above definition states, "an extraordinary event manifesting divine intervention in human affairs," our attention would be captured even if only for a few minutes. We would pause and take note. However, since the word 'miracle' has become such an overused description for common occurrences, when we hear the word, it just falls flat having no real impact on us. It is because we understand that saying something is a miracle is merely a figure of speech. Like during sports season when someone says it would be a miracle if a particular team won a game because they are not equally matched with their opponent. Everyone knows it wouldn't really be a 'miracle'…unusual maybe, but not anything truly supernatural.

[2] Miriam Webster Online Dictionary; first definition.

THE MIRACLE, THE WITNESSES AND ME

Many people do not hesitate to state that God performed a miracle in my life based on what they saw or heard about me when I was in the hospital, but not everyone is so quick to embrace that word. They assume, as I mentioned, that it's just a figure of speech until they hear some details. Others do not believe that there was a miracle because believing that a miracle occurred requires a belief in God or in something supernatural that is beyond their intellectual understanding or experiences. They are not willing to entertain that a miracle occurred because it would require, at a minimum, that they admit that areas they accepted as black and white may be grey or different than they thought. When I share with these people, I've seen the skeptical expressions, the polite silence, or the sympathetic look that says, "Awww, I thought she was smarter than that. Does she really believe in God and that Jesus performs miracles?!" Others, quickly start talking about how it was only medical prowess and drugs that got me from where I was when I entered the ICU to where I was when I left the hospital and beyond. For sure, there was a good team of doctors and nurses attending to me, but the thing about the 'it's all due to medicine' view is that none of the medical professionals involved in my case ever said to me that it was their medical expertise and processes that turned me around and restored me to where I am today. Instead, they admitted they did not have the answers and were trying all types of things because they were unsure. I recall my cousin Dari telling me that at one point when multiple tests were being administered that a doctor wanted to check my spine. She said to him "She walked into the hospital, so why would there be something wrong with her spine?" At that point, they did not know what to try. In fact, some who treated me in ICU were shocked when they later saw me in my patient room in the improved condition that I was in, so if they had expected my recovery, their reaction would not have been as it was. Sometimes those listening to my testimony would shift the focus to trying to figure out the reasons why my heart stopped in the first place (I must note that several of the doctors have said that they don't know why it happened or as one said, it was a combination of factors: a perfect storm). But, even if one could pinpoint the original cause or causes with certainty, that has nothing to do with the fact that my heart did indeed stop and other of my bodily functions shut down and that even with the aggressive help of people, it was divine intervention that brought me out of the situation, sustained me, and restored me far beyond anyone's expectation.

    The first person to use the term miracle to describe my situation was one of the doctors who had been on my team in the ICU. I then heard the term used by others who

THE MIRACLE, THE WITNESSES AND ME

saw me while in ICU and then afterward. I got used to their stares and their questions to assess whether there was some remaining incapacitation in me. Some just expressed their disbelief that I was cognizant and having a conversation when I had not been expected to survive the ICU. However, after reading my medical case notes, talking to medical folks, hearing eye-witness accounts from friends and family, reading articles about survival rates of people who experience some of the things I had, and most importantly living the full life I am living on a daily basis, I am comfortable using the word 'miracle' too. And, like the definition at the beginning of this chapter, when I use the word, I'm talking about an extraordinary event resulting from divine intervention. Yes, God has intervened to bring about the miraculous. I believe it because I'm living it.

Section II

Wales

FROM WALES TO A DC EMERGENCY ROOM

What was I doing in Wales you may ask? I went to attend a non-work, community focused conference where I was one of just a few Americans joining others from around the globe. On my journey by train from England to Wales, I texted pictures of the stunning green countryside with creamy colored sheep roaming freely to my childhood girlfriend Rosemary. I also sent pictures of the dramatic multi-hued sky over the marshy water to some other friends. In a text to one of them, I said "look at this pic of the day I was entering into the area. It was like the Glory of God was coming through the clouds." I was excited to be entering this beautiful land. I thoroughly enjoyed the sessions and meeting other attendees as well as the friendly locals I encountered during my brief time there. It was indeed an unforgettable experience.

I was scheduled to return to the states on November 20th and shortly before leaving Wales, I booked a hotel room in downtown DC for November 20th and 21st because it would be too late when I arrived on the 20th to travel another hour home to West Virginia. More importantly, I was feeling sick and wanted to schedule an appointment at

THE MIRACLE, THE WITNESSES AND ME

an urgent care facility on November 21st. I was so sick during the final days of my trip in Wales that I considered seeking medical help while I was there. In fact, due to an unrelenting cough that I had, I was also encouraged by two women who were attending the conference and staying in the same guest house as me, to see a nurse while I was there. One of the women, a nurse herself, gave me a phone number I could call and describe my symptoms and get advice on whether I should see a doctor or go to the hospital, or just rest. The number was written on a small piece of paper. I remember sitting on the edge of the bed, staring at the number debating whether I should call and playing out in my head what would happen if I did call. I turned the piece of paper over in my hands for what seemed like an hour. I felt very strongly that I had to wait and seek medical care in the United States rather than in Wales. Although the woman assured me that the medical services would be very good, and I didn't doubt her word, I knew that I had to go home; I was convinced of it. I have to say that thinking through the journey home in my head seemed overwhelming given how I was feeling. I would take a taxi from the guest house to the train station in Wales, take a train to another town in Wales, take a second train to London, take a taxi in London to a hotel I booked to stay overnight, take a taxi in the morning to London's Heathrow

Airport, fly from London to Iceland for a short layover, take another plane from Iceland to Washington, DC, and take a taxi from that airport to the hotel! Yeah...it was a lot all while carrying and pulling luggage and walking from place to place which was becoming increasingly harder for me. Despite all of this, I thought to myself that I could not end up in a hospital in Wales though I did not specifically know why I felt so strongly about that. So, I placed the paper with the phone number in a book, prayed asking Jesus to watch over me, strengthen me for the journey, and went to sleep. The next morning, I felt much better and someone who I rode with to one of the conference sessions the day before even mentioned that I looked like I was back to myself. I was stronger, yes, and the cough I had the day before had subsided, but I was not back to myself; I still was not well. I knew I would schedule an appointment as soon as possible after landing in the US.

What I know now is that the reason I did not have peace about calling the phone number I had been given and why I felt it was imperative for me to make it home for treatment rather than possibly ending up in a hospital in Europe around strangers was because there were a host of people who needed to witness and participate in the miracle that God was going to perform in my life.

A 'RED HERRING': WHAT OCCURRED BEFORE NOVEMBER 21ST?

At some point when you are reading this book, you may be wondering "Hey, what happened between the time when you left Wales, and you arrived in DC and landed in the Emergency Room?" Good Question. Afterall, we are not talking about a short 4-hour trip. No, not at all. It was more like 30 hours of travel via three train rides and two flights not counting the layovers in between and then four taxis. In fact, you may be thinking "Let's go back even before you were in Wales. Did something just go "Poof" and happen to you while you were there?" Were you sick before you went? Were you clueless about what was going on with your body?[3] These are logical questions but please bear with me while I digress for a moment. In the practice of law, sometimes one of the parties in a dispute will add an argument in its Complaint[4] that is not the real issue of the controversy. The purpose of making the argument is to distract the other side so they will spend time and resources.

---

[3] My good friend Monet said to me "that's not like you, you're always in tune with what's happening in your body. I don't get it."
[4] The initial pleading (document) that gets things started in a court of law.

THE MIRACLE, THE WITNESSES AND ME

researching that issue instead of focusing on the more principal issues that are critical to an outcome. Attorneys sometimes refer to this unimportant side argument as a *red herring* because it serves as a distraction and takes the attention away from crucial issue(s).

You may be thinking "Why does she bring this up… the red herring thing?" It is because as I mentioned in my beginning comments, this book is about what occurred on November 21st and beyond…the miracles from that period and the witnesses of the miracles. It is not that I can't provide details about facts leading up to and during my journey back to the US, but there is no power in recounting facts just to satisfy curiosity. You see, those events do not add to, take away from, or answer the critical issues related to 'what' God did in the ICU and beyond, the people who witnessed or heard what was going on and participated in the process, or the impact the miracle had on me and others. Since that information is not part of this testimony, the answers to those questions and any related discussion are not important or *red herrings*. So, the omission of details of the pre-November 21st events is intentional because I don't want to distract from what is important in this testimony.

SECTION III

THE MIRACLE: STRATEGIC POSITIONING

STRATEGIC POSITIONING EMERGENCY ROOM

In my view, God strategically positioned key people on November 21, 2021, in preparation for what was to come: nothing was just luck. My cousin Donne', who is like a sister, took on the role of my representative when she arrived at the ICU after her sister Dari told her that I was there. *Donne' was strategic person number one.* Brenda, a friend from college, was one of the first people Donne' called to talk about my condition. *Brenda was strategic person number two.* When going over the events of the night in the ICU, she mentioned that she just happened to be in a store in the Washington DC area to buy a table for a Thanksgiving dinner she was having the next day. Since Brenda was in the DC area, she was able to let my dear friend Linda who lived in DC know I was in the hospital, and they could quickly head to the emergency room together to see me. *Linda was strategic person number three.* The two of them were able to make it to the emergency room in much less time than it would have taken had Brenda been at home near Baltimore, MD where she lived. Had she been there, it could have taken her about an hour to get to DC to pick up Linda instead of the 15 - 20 minutes that it took her because she just 'happened to be' in a DC suburb buying the table.

Brenda and Linda started praying once they heard about my situation and called on others to do the same. Linda would later be instrumental in setting up one prayer group and informing everyone about prayer points and how my condition was progressing. Donne' also called Elaine who I've known since kindergarten or before and is close friends with me and Donne'. *Elaine was strategic person number four*! Elaine has told me more than once that she still does not understand the quickness with which she was able to travel the congested highways of Northern Virginia to get to the ER in Washington, DC shaving off 20 minutes in travel time. A trip that could have taken more than 40 minutes took half that amount of time. Elaine, as I explain later, is the doctor you want in your corner when in a critical situation!

I'm convinced that it was God's strategic positioning of the right individuals that would be key in the story that would unfold. Before I go on, let me back up a bit.

STRATEGIC POSITIONING:
The Hotel Pickup & Urgent Care

On the morning of November 21st, the day after I had returned from Europe, I called an Urgent Care clinic in Downtown DC to schedule an appointment. While I waited for a call back about a time for an appointment, I sent a text to my cousin Dari telling her that I was trying to schedule a doctor's appointment and wanted to know if she could give me a ride. Dari lives in New York but was home in DC for Thanksgiving. I told her that I was too weak to come to her parents' house and navigate the multiple steps there. I called her later to let her know the time of my appointment; she and her husband Robert arrived at the hotel in ample time to take me to the Urgent Care clinic. Had Dari and Robert not been available, I would have had to catch an Uber or Taxi which I originally planned to do before I thought to call her. Who knows how that would have gone but God was in control of the situation; they were available and happy to pick me up.[5]

---

[5] Months after I was released from the hospital and was talking to my friend Fay, she told me she said to Dari "It was good that you were able to take her to the hospital. What would have happened if you hadn't taken her?" They both looked at each other as that question hung in the air. That question of "what would have happened if...?" applied to so

I really liked the doctor at the Urgent Care clinic who examined me and still remembers how very thorough and kind she was. As the doctor examined me, she was cool as a cucumber but obviously concerned. I could tell that she did not want to alarm me when she told me that my heart rate was extremely high. She told me I needed to go to the hospital right away and asked if I had a preference about which hospital. There was a hospital I thought I wanted to go to because it was small and then another one that was close to where we were and that had a good reputation. The hospital I went to was neither of the ones I had considered. Once the decision was made based on her recommendation, she told us that she was calling ahead to let them know I was coming. Off we went, Dari, Robert, and I, on our way to the ER. None of us knew what was to come. When we arrived at the hospital, it was obvious that the urgent care doctor forewarned them of the severity of my condition because as soon as I approached the window to check-in and provided my name, I was ushered back right away.

many points along the way. The real question was, what would have happened if God had not been in the mix! What would have happened if I had gone to the hospital in Wales? What would have happened if I had gotten sicker on the plane or during a layover while I was travelling back to the U.S.? What would have happened if I had fallen out in the hotel room? And...on and on. But God's promise that He would never leave or forsake me continued to unfold over and over again throughout the journey from Wales to the U.S.!

STRATEGIC POSITIONING: The First Call for Prayer

I prayed while I was sick in Wales and during my entire journey home to the U.S. I even asked for prayer before I travelled out of the country as is my habit to do. But my request to some people to pray for me on the night of November 21st when I was in the ER was critical and the beginning of the onslaught of prayers that would follow in hours, days, and weeks to come. While I sat in the triage area waiting for next steps and not knowing that my friends and family were on their way, I sent the following text message to six people: "**PRAY… IN ER.**" It was a simple request, and I provided no further clarity. I did not have time. I had to set up a hedge of prayer right away. Although a couple of them asked what was going on or whether I was in the ER with someone else who was sick, or whether it was me that was being seen, I did not have time to say more than I had. I felt confident that those that received the text would pray even without having details. Included among those that I sent the message to were Merilyn (a minister and Elder at my church, my pastor's wife and my friend); Sheila (a minister and Elder at my church and friend); Patrice (a minister and friend); Temaki (a minister and friend); and Linda (a friend since college and my Godson's mother). The atmosphere for the miracles that would occur was being established as prayers were already going forth.

It was critical that before the medical procedures and treatments began, prayers were in motion to set the atmosphere.

STRATEGIC POSITIONING:
Medical Personnel

The right people were in position in the ER to do what needed to be done from a medical perspective. In the months...years following my ordeal, my childhood girlfriend Rosemary who always is close by when something major happens in my life has mentioned to me on more than one occasion that I had the right people around me to make decisions and how important that was. She said that it was a good thing that my cousin Donne' allowed people to visit me. What she may not have known was, that even before those people had arrived at the hospital, prayer had already begun. Indeed, I attribute the right people being in the right place, at the right time making the right medical decisions to be the result of God's mercy and divine plan.

After being in the triage of the ER for what seemed like a long to me, I told my cousin Dari that there was no need for her to stay with me and that she and her husband could stay in my hotel room if they wanted since it was paid for. I handed her my watch and my grandfather's ring and encouraged her to leave. When she left the ER, she called her sister Donne' to let her know I was in the emergency room. Donne' immediately left where she was and made her way to the hospital. A couple of years later she would tell me that on that night she was in the middle of a visit with a dear friend. As mentioned at the beginning of this section, one of the people my cousin called was Elaine, a close childhood friend; like family, who is also a physician. In a text message about 30 minutes after she left me in the ER, Dari told me that Donne' and Elaine were on their way to me. Donne' was coming from DC and Elaine was coming from Virginia. I mentioned earlier that Elaine made it to the ICU in half the time it should have taken. God was going to use her!

Elaine is one of those doctors whose greatest gift as a medical professional is not what was learned in medical school. Don't get me wrong, she is a technically skilled and sought-after physician who has been recognized in her profession throughout her career. But, in my opinion, that special *something* that Elaine possesses and that distinguishes her from her peers cannot be taught. Elaine is able to discern things…to sense what is going on with a patient when others with a similar medical background would need to perform an extensive examination to catch up with Elaine's intuitive assessment. I periodically tell her that she is gifted by God and this gift was in full operation the night that I was in ICU. As I sat there with my vitals being taken and responding to questions, Elaine told me that she looked at me and could tell that I was about to 'code'[6]. In one of our conversations after being out of the hospital, she told me that she went to the emergency medical team and told them concerning me: "You need to get your code blue team together right now because she is about to code!" Elaine said the team looked at her as though she was crazy and questioned who she was. Mind you, she was not a physician at that hospital and had no medical privileges there. Elaine recited her medical credentials then very strongly and persuasively told them; warned them really, that they needed to act right away. She boldly told these doctors who were on staff what they needed to do because of what she observed going on with me. They were looking at me as well and did not see what she saw. They would have been within their rights to boot her out and tell Elaine to mind her business because they were in charge, but that is not what happened at all. They did as she said and started getting the team together. That in

---

[6] WebMD states that "there's no formal definition for a code, but doctors often use the term as slang for a cardiopulmonary arrest happening to a patient in a hospital or clinic, requiring a team of providers (sometimes called a code team) to rush to the specific location and begin immediate resuscitative efforts." https://www.webmd.com.

itself was amazing; definitely not normal. A couple of years after that night I sent Elaine a text message thanking her for being there for me. It certainly wasn't the first time that I had thanked her, but I did it again. She responded saying "Charlma, being there for you was what needed to be done. The thing that was hard was getting on that plane and leaving knowing you were here." God knew who would need to be in ER for me and the amount of time they needed to be there. Elaine was strategically positioned to be there when she was. It was fine that she had to leave to catch a flight to see her family in Ohio for Thanksgiving because her assignment had been accomplished. Truly God was in control of the process!

I'm told that the code blue team included a strong tall guy weighing more than two hundred pounds who was assigned to perform CPR. He was said to be one of the best if not the best at what he did. Just as my friend had predicted, within minutes of them assembling the code blue team, my heart stopped. What I remember before my heart stopping, was someone laying me back from my upright position and me feeling like I was drowning. I heard 'there she goes' and I have no further recollection. Thanks to Elaine, the team was immediately ready to go. I'm told that deep chest compressions from the 'big guy' were applied consistently for 5 minutes, 10 minutes,

15 minutes without it having any effect. I am told that he seemed to be pushing down on my chest with all of his force. At one point, after 15 minutes of intense chest compressions, someone recommended that the CPR be stopped because nothing was happening. The person asked the question "How long are you going to continue...I think you should stop." But the doctor in charge said that he was not going to stop! He said that since I had walked into the ICU, he was not going to let me die on his watch. There is no universal protocol for administering CPR in an emergency room setting in the United States that states that CPR should be administered for X number of minutes. It is left to the discretion of the medical professional in charge who considers various factors. The CPR continued and after 20 minutes, there was still no pulse. I was told months later by Elaine that she just knew that I would have many broken bones in my chest because of the great force used by the very large technician administering CPR and because of the length of time that it continued. God shielded and preserved me because I did not have any broken bones and never had any chest pains. The CPR continued and 21, 22, 23 minutes passed with no pulse.

The CPR technician and the doctor in charge were other examples of strategic positioning because... after 26 minutes, my heart started beating again! Thanks be to God who was in control and guiding the procedures!

STRATEGIC POSITIONING: The Security Officer and his Wife

Dari told me that she did not come back to the hospital the night they dropped be off after hearing about my condition because she thought it was best for her to stay with her elderly mother (my aunt) rather than leaving her in the house alone and confused that everyone was gone. It would have been extremely disorienting. I also believe that hearing that her cousin (other big sister) was not expected to make it through the night may have influenced her decision to stay with her mother because she would have had to be the one to let her know if I passed away. When Dari and her husband Robert came back to the ICU the next day to see me, they stopped at the desk to find out where I was. They gave the guard at the desk my name and he said "I know her, she is a minister at my church! I did not know she was sick." What is the likelihood of that happening that the guard responsible for entry knew me? I know that once he found out that he prayed for me! His wife, a dear Christian sister, was a nurse at the hospital where I was and would later visit me in ICU.

Although she was not assigned to care for me, I was told that she was protective of me and the care I was receiving. On one of her visits when I was still in ICU but off of the ventilator, I recall her coming and showing me so much tenderness and attention. My mouth was very parched, and she put a sponge in water and put it on my lips. Wow! That gesture was everything to me at that time. Even as I write this, I can recall how satisfying that was. I will never forget that visit! If her husband had not been the guard on duty on the day my cousin came, who knows whether she would have ever found out that I was there. God was strategic even in the little things!

> *"God's Timing and Positioning of People Is Strategic."*

SECTION IV
THE MIRACLE | PRAYER

PRAYER- Powerful Part of The Process

Communicating with God through prayer is powerful and ignites action. The Bible says that "The heartfelt and persistent prayer of a righteous man (believer) is able to accomplish much [when put into action and made effective by God—it is dynamic and can have tremendous power]."[7] In another passage, God invites His people to pray and lets them know that He will answer.[8] Prayer was indeed the powerful force that surrounded my situation; it was at the center of what was going on as people prayed for my life to be spared, for Jesus to heal my body, the doctors and nurses to be guided, and for strength for those who came to see me. The prayers preceded the miracle and were a way for those on earth to join with what was being done in Heaven!

In the ICU, not only was I prayed for, but others were prayed for as well. My pastor told me that when he

---

[7] James 5:16 (Amplified).
[8] Just one of many examples is II Chronicles 7:14 "if my people who are called by my name humble themselves and pray and seek my face and turn from their wicked ways, then I will hear from heaven and will forgive their sin and heal their land."

came to see me, he felt sure that God was not ready to take me; that it was not my time to die. He said that once he had that assurance, he shifted his attention and started praying for the doctors and nurses on duty. Someone else told me that on one night when she was there as prayers and singing were going on, one of the nurses asked for prayer. Another friend told me that with people coming and going in shifts in the ICU that she wanted to be on the shift when the people who were praying were going to be there! She knew that something powerful was happening in that ICU room.

Several people have shared with me that they also prayed for others during the times when they visited me. Did everyone who visited me pray? No, of course not. There were some who did not pray, nor did they believe in prayer in terms of communicating with God... calling on the name of Jesus. They came simply to see me and talk to me, and I greatly appreciate those visits. But it never takes 'everyone' doing something to get things done! The Bible says when just two or three people are gathered together in God's name, He is in the midst![9] What Is certain is that those who did pray were part of something life-changing not only for me, but for them and

[9] Matthew 18:20.

others as well. They saw God's response to prayers, and many were strengthened in the process. Yes, prayer was a constant theme…a common denominator in my story.

> *"Through prayer, heaven and earth connect."*

> "This illness isn't meant to end in death. It's for God's glory, so that the Son of God may be glorified through it."
> John 11:4

BRANCHES GOING EVERYWHERE

Picture a tree with branches, that have branches, that have still more branches. That is how the prayers for me can be visualized; like a tree with branches going everywhere. Prayer was going forth from different groups of people and some groups were connected to each while others were distinct from the other groups. However, at some point, the various groups began to converge such as when people who knew me from different stages of my life were at the ICU at the same time or when the information about my condition, primarily shared by Linda, spread among the groups.

As mentioned earlier, my cousin Donne' set things in motion when she called a few people when I was admitted to ICU which led to my family and friends in Ohio praying. Linda who I've known since college and came to the ICU with Brenda the night I was admitted, led one branch where she painstakingly sent out regular updates on my condition and sent focused prayer requests via e-mails, text messages and phone calls to a group of about 15 people who then forwarded this information, or portions of it to groups that they were connected to. In one message she said "Charlma was really opening her eyes as Janice read scriptures and played videos from everyone. Keep it coming." Although she sent updates to people in other prayer branches, there was a core group of people who she asked to pray about certain aspects of my condition. In one text message Linda specifically asked for prayer for my kidneys as I was receiving dialysis treatment at that time. Linda was particular about who was part of that group. She wanted them to believe in the healing power of Jesus.

On this point, she told me about a concerned work colleague of mine who asked her to send him updates. She told him that she had a group that she sent regular updates to but told him that she would send him separate updates because she didn't think he would want to be part of that particular group. Being a persistent lawyer who knew how to get answers, he asked why he couldn't be part of the group she referred to. He told her that he did want to be part of that group to receive updates. Linda tried to beat around the bush saying "Well...I'll just provide you an update." When he tried to find out what it was about 'the group' she finally said, "That group is praying for Charlma!" He responded right away telling her that he believed in prayer, wanted to receive those updates and that he would know who to share them with.

Another prayer branch was through my church at the time, the Outpouring Worship and Life Center.[10] My church had a 24-hour prayer chain where members signed up to pray for one-hour slots. I recall my cousin Dari telling me that she got chills when she saw the messages about how they were praying for me. It warmed my heart when I looked at some of the text messages during that time. There was such excitement about ensuring that all of the prayer shifts were covered! The following are a few texts from Milly, the prayer leader:

> Good morning…just 3 shifts remain!!!

> I am pleased to announce that Monday is almost fully covered except 1-3 p.m. Tuesday only needs 1-4 p.m. covered & Wednesday 9

> Wow…just Wow!!! She's completely covered!!! All shifts are

Another branch of the prayer tree was started by Patrice and Temaki, two of my friends who are fellow missionaries and ministers of the Gospel who I met when we travelled to Africa a decade ago. This branch resulted in people in Africa, Asia, the Middle East, and Europe partnering through prayer. Patrice and Temaki were the

---

[10] There is a separate section about The Outpouring Worship and Life Center.

people who I texted when I arrived in the ICU asking them to pray. In fact, I had asked them to pray for me before I even went to Wales. However, their branch of the prayer tree that stretched to other nations came about when a friend from my church contacted Patrice and, speaking about me and the severity of my situation, said to her, "Sis, we almost lost her!" I had only introduced Patrice to my friend about 6 months earlier because of commonalities between their ministries and because I thought Patrice and her husband Frank, and my friend and his wife should meet. That introduction ended up being critical in my process because if my friend had not contacted Patrice, I don't know how she would have found out about my illness and set the global branch of the prayer tree in motion. Patrice contacted Temaki, Temaki contacted Bishop Clifton Clarke, a mentor and friend who contacted some of my friends and ministry partners in the Philippines, Pastors Danny and Leah Ragudo, whom I had introduced him to some years before when we traveled there. They told others including a young woman from their church who was living and working in Saudi Arabia. Temaki also contacted Cornelius Ibrahim, an Evangelist and friend from Northern Ghana who calls me mother. Temaki also sought prayers from her ministry partners in Belgium. I am convinced that God set things in place far in advance of my illness through the introduction of Patrice and my friend because![11]

Another branch of the prayer tree went out through my good friend Phillipa. When Phillipa heard the news from Linda, she was out of town helping to care for her mother who was extremely ill and celebrating Thanksgiving with her family. Talking to her two years after my ordeal, Philippa reflected on where she was and what she was doing at the time she got the call about my condition. She said she looked at her mother's small frame in the bed that she was not able to get out of, and then as Phillipa reflected on the words she heard during that phone call about me, she looked back at her mother and said "No." In other words, she did not want to accept that what was occurring to her mother was also destined to happen with me. She, her daughter Kaila, and the rest of her family prayed for me. Since Phillipa and I worked together for most of my career, past co-workers were notified through her. She contacted friends from my prior workplace to inform them about what was going on with me. They prayed and asked others to pray as well.

---

[11] One text message from Linda to some she asked to pray stated that I "was blessed with a visit from missionary Temaki Carr. She first met Charlma on a mission trip to Ghana...Charlma is being prayed worldwide..all pastors, missionaries, people in villages in the Philippines, Ghana, Kenya and Belgium are praying day and night."

From this group, Ogo a friend and co-worker who I worked with at my prior workplace and then years later at my current place of employment was informed through this branch of the prayer tree. She then notified my current co-workers and provided them current information about what was going on including connecting my manager to my family and my friend Linda who kept him up to date with my status. One of my co-workers sent the following prayer to be read for me:

> *"Lord, you invite all who are burdened to come to you. Allow your healing hand to heal Charlma. Most loving Jesus bring Charlma health in body and spirit. Touch gently this life which have created now and forever."*

The prayer tree quickly expanded and as mentioned, prayer was occurring on four continents. I mention some of the main branches, but there were so many others like family and friends from my birthplace in Ohio, and those in the town where I currently live who prayed after hearing about me being in the hospital through my friend and landlord Renee and another neighbor who noticed that she hadn't seen me walking around town which led her to enquire about my whereabouts. The following are text messages in my phone from two friends in my town to my cousin Donne' or to me:

- *Hello, this is...from Harpers Ferry. I'm a friend...Just want you to know that my family and I are praying...I will also get my friends who she met at my house and my church family praying for her...Asking God's blessings on all.*
- *Are you gaining strength? Praying for you every day...*

Even after I was out of ICU people continued to pray for me. One visit from five of my colleagues from my current workplace will always be special to me. I was so surprised and happy to see them, and I am glad I was in a state where I was fully aware that they came and could appreciate the gift and card they brought. One of them who I directly work with saw me and nodded as though seeing me let him know I was going to be alright. Another one was testing me a little by making eating motions, I think to remind me that we used to always share gummy bears when we were in the office. Two of the women looked concerned but tried to be strong.

Before they left, they held hands around my bed as one of them led a prayer for me. I did not expect that, and it truly blessed me because it was one of the first times that I saw people praying for me. It is not possible to share about all the people who prayed for me and there are many that I'll never know about. When I returned to work, someone who I know but do not work directly with said to me in passing "There were people pulling for you that you don't even know!" I've heard similar comments from other people, even some who I did not personally know. They would say "So and so asked me to pray for you" or "Are you the one who almost died that we were praying for?"

Although I have no idea who was praying for me, and it is not my business to know, I do know that God responds to prayer and responded to those for me.

> *"Community prayer connects those praying to God and to each other and activates change."*

THE ICU BECAME A PLACE FOR PRAYER AND PRAISE AROUND MY BED

At different points through my life, I have visited loved ones in the ICU. I would hesitantly approach the door where visitors were buzzed in, not knowing what awaited me on the other side but knowing it was not good; it was the ICU after all. The mood was always somber…heavy. The area would be quiet except for the beeping sounds of equipment monitoring the vital signs of those who occupied the beds. Perhaps groans or whimpers could be heard from those patients cognizant enough to release them. Or there might be cries from loved ones who had lost hope. The probability of impending death was always a thought not too far off. In my case, I heard about the wailing or muffled cries of some friends and family in the halls outside my room, in the visitor's area, and in the room where I was as well. This mood made sense to me and was familiar to what my experiences had been when I visited the sick in ICU. But I would find out that these familiar sounds and expressions were not the only ones occurring in the ICU during my stay there. There was something quite different that was also going on!

THE MIRACLE, THE WITNESSES AND ME

I have heard repeated reports about the prayers and songs of praise that were going on around my bed and the surrounding area. When people typically think about singing songs of praise to God, most would immediately think about this activity occurring in a traditional setting like a church or a chapel or at least during some religious ceremony. But many who visited me understand that God is ever present, not restricted to spaces and places, and is always worthy of praise and honor! Therefore, praying or praising God while washing dishes or cradling a child is in order and has the same effect as doing so during a church service with the accompaniment of an organ. One powerful thing that many people gained during the 2020-22 period of the COVID-19 pandemic when movements were greatly restricted and many church buildings closed for varying periods of time, is the understanding that going to a physical church building was not necessary to experience the power and presence of God. And so it was that the ICU area around my bed became a place of praise. I was told by several people that in addition to praying for my recovery, talking to me, and crying because of what was going on with me there were some who boldly lifted up the name of Jesus and sang praises! Some of my friends told me that when medical predictions about my chances of survival and likely diminished capacity were spoken, they were empowered and determined to pray and sing to counteract those negative reports. One friend said that she had to take authority over the atmosphere in the ICU and speak the Word of God as opposed to reacting to the grim reports that she heard.

My childhood friend Rosemary recorded one of those praise sessions and showed it to me about a year after I had gotten out of the hospital. My first reaction when I saw my image in the video was "I look dead!" I had tubes coming from everywhere and a non-responsive gaze. Even to this day it takes my breath away when I look at the image. Despite how I looked, this setting around my ICU bed became a place where praise replaced tears. Rosemary's video shows my Godbrother Eric and my friends Patrice and Temaki standing around my bed. Temaki had her cell phone in her hand playing music and singing as Eric and Patrice joined in. Eric is known for many things including his great generosity and determination, but one thing he is not known for is singing or even being able to carry a tune for that matter! But he wasn't singing to impress anyone but rather he was praising Jesus giving it all he had. As the music played, he can be heard singing "He is my comfort" as he rubbed my leg over the cover and swayed from side to side. It was heartfelt and blesses me so when I see it. The recording was short but so sweet and powerful. The powerful aspect is that in the face of how I looked, the three of them could still pray and sing. They were obviously focused on God to whom they prayed and praised, not on me. Otherwise, they would have been silenced by the grim sight in front of them. That video is a gift, I am so thankful to Rosemary for recording it.

Another example of singing in the ICU was during one of Patrice and Frank's hospital visits when Tim, a friend and one of the young ministers at my church was also visiting. Based on Patrice's account, it seemed to me like there was a worship service going on at that time as well. She said that Tim sang and that she and Frank prayed. She mentioned that visit to me on more than one occasion because she was really moved by Tim. She said, "he was such a worshipper!" At some point after I was released from the hospital, I asked Tim in a text message whether he remembered singing in the ICU while Patrice and Frank were praying, and he responded Yes! When I relayed how moved Patrice was by his singing, Tim and I had the following lighthearted exchange:

> **Tim:** "😂 *well praise the Lord...We both know it wasn't my voice, lol"*

Me: *"So…you were obviously under the anointing!"*

Tim: *"Lol, amen! Holy Spirit was clearly at work in that place, so I will certainly not take anything away from that!"*

Some of the praises that occurred were not in person, but via technology. Niya, a worship leader and my girlfriend Darla's daughter whose powerful voice commands one to turn their focus to the heavens, sang on the phone as it was lifted to my ear. I am told that everyone listening in the ICU was impacted by her offering. A young Evangelist from a village in Northern Ghana sent a recording of songs sung by young women in his ministry that I am told was played for me. My friend Maria sent a couple of Samoan gospel songs to be played for me. She asked me some months after I left the hospital whether I heard the songs saying she really wanted me to hear them. I have no recollection of hearing them. However, the sounds of praise permeated the atmosphere of my ICU area and blessed those who heard them.

My friend Janice told me on more than one occasion about an evening when people from my church were praying for me and some of the nurses started asking for prayer as well. I have heard that from others too. Yes, the atmosphere was one where praises and prayers were taking place and many people wanted to be a part.

> "The right place to pray and praise God is wherever You are."

LET IT FLOW LIKE THE RIVER JORDAN: SPECIFIC PRAYER REQUESTS

"[b] Bartimaeus, the son of Timaeus, sat by the highway side begging. And when he heard that it was Jesus of Nazareth, he began to cry out, and say Jesus, 'thou Son of David, have mercy on me...And Jesus answered and said unto him, What do you want me to do for you? The blind man said unto him, Lord, that I might receive my sight." Mark 10: 46-47, 51.

As seen in the scriptural account above, a blind man named Bartimaeus who was sitting by the road when he heard a crowd of people and realized that they were following after Jesus, excitedly cried out "have mercy on me!" He did not specifically say what he wanted but simply asked Jesus to have mercy on him. Jesus, however, asked Bartimaeus for details saying, "what do you want me to do for you?" It was in response to this question that Bartimaeus made a specific request and said "Lord, I want to see again!"

As the doctors shared their prognoses about my condition, Linda would send out specific prayer requests to address the areas discussed by the doctors and to counteract their predictions. One area of prayer focus concerned my kidneys which were among the several organs that had basically shut down. I was told I was too weak to be transferred to the location where dialysis took place in the hospital, so I was administered dialysis at my bedside in the ICU. I was told it was a slow process and for a couple of days, it did not yield the desired results. Some of the medical personnel expressed frustration to one of my friends because my body was not responding to the dialysis as the doctors wanted and my kidneys were not independently working. Just like Bartimaeus in the Bible who asked Jesus to address a specific problem, people started specifically praying for my kidneys. Linda told me that my friend Darla said she was asking God to let the urine flow out of my kidneys like the river Jordan!

The next day when Linda went to the ICU, the doctor excitedly told her that he did not know what was happening because the urine was flowing so much that it was hard to stop! She responded "Oh, we've been praying for that!" She said the doctor's response was to tell everyone they could stop praying about that and to shift their attention to another area! Months later, Linda showed me a picture she had taken of the bag full of urine after their focused prayer. She took the picture as a memorial of what God had done. Just like Jesus restoring Bartimaeus's sight after he specifically asked for that healing, a specific prayer went out for my kidneys and Jesus specifically responded!

> *"We should not hesitate to be specific when we pray."*

WHEN PRAYERS ARE ANSWERED, SOME PEOPLE ARE PERPLEXED

A friend shared the good news about my dramatic recovery with some people she had asked to pray for me when I was in ICU. She told them she had just seen me at an event and that I looked great. They responded "You asked us to pray! I thought you said she was on life support!" She told them that yes, I had been on life-support, but God worked a miracle! They looked confused. Even though they had prayed, they did not really expect me to get better because I had been in a coma, so they were thrown off when the good news was shared about how God had answered the prayers. It didn't register for them. On another occasion, I was out at a reception with a friend, and someone asked her how I was doing because they, like so many others, had been asked to pray for me. When my friend pointed towards me and said, "there she is," the person said "No, I mean your friend that was in critical condition." In response, my friend said, yes…that is her. Again, there was a look of disbelief. At that event, I had noticed a person staring at me, but I wasn't sure why. I feel comfortable saying that anyone who prays whether regularly or on occasion, has experienced the disappointment of praying for something that did not occur in the way they wanted. It could have been a prayer that a family member or friend would be healed; but they were not. Or perhaps it was repeated prayers for the protection of our families, and then somewhere along the way, something tragic happens to a family member. So, when people were asked to pray for me in my critical state, especially during the initial stages, deep inside there were many who did not believe that I would survive, or that if I did, I would not be fully functional. That is why there were surprised or confused reactions from some of these people when they saw me out and about a couple of months after I was on the brink of death. I get it. Many had been down this road before, praying, believing, expecting yet being disappointed. Although some of these people were followers of Jesus Christ, the miracle worker, Christians can sometimes find themselves in a position of just going through the motions of praying...reciting words, without truly expecting the outcome they are praying for because of past disappointments. No one has answers to the age-old question of why certain prayers are answered while others are not. Regardless of your experience with prayer, my message is simple: Please do not stop believing! Do not stop praying! Do not allow past disappointments to shape your approach to prayer, because the loud and clear message from my situation is that God does answer prayers and still works miracles. That fact is undeniable because I am alive!

> *"Prayer should not be reduced to a religious ritual. Prayer rooted in faith always has impact even when the outcome of a situation is different than desired."*

"Miracles are never just for the recipient; they are also for all those who witness the miracle. The miracle can strengthen, encourage, and change the perspective of the witnesses. The question is, what will we do with what has been witnessed?"

SECTION V

THE MIRACLE: WITNESSES

WHAT THEY SAID

People's reactions, expressions, and comments to me in the months after leaving the hospital until now include some of the following:

"I call that a second breath of life...going in His strength now...doing the greater...more than you can ask or think!!" Larry Robbins

"You are a walking, talking miracle!" Clifton Clarke

I said "No, not Charlma...uh...uh." "I knew God wasn't finished with you yet. I knew you would make it through." Samuel Alan Burroughs

"I thought we were going to lose you girlfriend." Chef J

"There was no strategy for what I saw going on in the ICU. A person could not plan for it. It wasn't clear what I was to do!" Justin Wilson

"We just knew you were going to have broken bones from the CPR...that guy was big, and tall and used all of his force pounding on your chest." Linda Elaine Coleman

"I was on assignment. God told me to go see you and worship. I heard them say that you were not responding...that they might take you off of life support and I said, 'It's time for me to worship more!'" Temaki Carr

"We basically were told to prepare to say good-bye. Me and Max definitely wanted to come and say bye." Deb A

"You are a miracle! You were dead...and now you're alive." Dr. ____

"You're going to be stronger than you were before." Jamel

"I'm surprised there isn't a medical journal article about you."   Rosemary Duffy-Cooper

"I'm trying to figure out whether you were on my mind at that time; whether I prayed for you...was I part of that miracle?" Shantell

"I knew you would recover with all of the love that was in the room." Oyamiawa

"I believed God was going to bring you through but not that you'd be like this...doing everything...fully functioning like this... so quickly!"

"People were coming in shifts, I wanted to come when the people were there praying and singing. That's the shift I wanted!" Brenda Jackson

"It was like a church service in the ICU...it was something!" Aleia

THE WITNESSES

This Section talks about some of the people who came to see me in the ICU and/or in my Hospital Room. Most would call them 'visitors,' but I call them witnesses. There are others who I talk about who I also call witnesses even though they just heard about what I went through and did not see me until I was released from the hospital. Though those in this second group were not directly involved in my ordeal, some of them still have a story to tell. Since only my family was supposed to visit me in the ICU, I'm told that during the initial week some of my close friends were saying that they were my sibling or a cousin. After hearing this from multiple people, it did not take long for the nurses to realize that it was highly unlikely that my family was that big! They nonetheless were very lenient and allowed people to come, probably thinking that given my condition, anyone who came should be given the opportunity to see me. I am so thankful for that! There were other people who did not pretend to be my relatives but simply said they were there to see me. Some of them described their ability to come back and forth to see me whenever they wanted as the grace of God.

I have been told that people came in shifts to the ICU and that many times, because of the number of people coming, some had to wait for others to leave before they could enter. In addition to family, my friends from childhood, college, and law school came. Colleagues from work; current and past, ministry partners and church members came as well. These precious people flew in, took trains, buses or drove. They had been beckoned. Some were encouraged to come see me, for what might be the last time, since I was not expected to survive. The night that I arrived at the Emergency Room, some like my Godbrother Eric and my girlfriend Rosemary received phone calls telling them that I might not make it through the night. Eric said that he was in the middle of dinner with some of his family when he got the call about me and they just started praying. He said he then called his Godson, a pastor, so that he could pray too. Eric flew from Ohio to DC the next day to be with me. After I had made it through the first night and the following nights, friends and family were encouraged to come to let me hear their voice with the hope that it would bring me out of the medically induced coma I was in. Some people came just to sit with me without any specific agenda. The paths of the different groups crossed; they started becoming familiar with each other and learning things about me from each other that they previously did not know.

Someone told me that it was though there were parts of my life, they had no idea about until they talked to people who knew me from a different context. Some of these people still ask me about some of those they meet. My friend Fay told me "it was like we became family. It was good."

Witnesses to an event are important. They see things, interpret what they see, and sometimes consciously hold on to what they experienced to make sure they don't forget. The Gospels of Matthew, Mark, Luke, and John are made up entirely of witness accounts. These followers of Jesus Christ, his disciples, walked along side of Him seeing the miracles He performed first-hand, listening to His teaching, and experiencing His touch. They were impacted by what they witnessed, and their lives were never the same. The disciples told others about Jesus, who told others, who told others and so on. Witness testimony in a court of law, especially the testimony of eyewitnesses, can change the tide of a legal case because these are people who can tell what they saw with their own eyes. They are not just repeating a story that someone told them. And then, if more than one witness can speak about the same event, the credibility of what is being shared increases. Although they did not know it at the time, the people who were with me in the Emergency Room, ICU, or my hospital room and who later saw my recovery at different stages such as being cleared to return to work the same month I was released from the hospital, or hiking for 11 miles 5 months after being released are witnesses! Witnesses have testified about the power of God, others have testified about how they were personally impacted, and still others who have simply said what they saw and heard without attributing their observations to the God who still performs miracles.

What have the witnesses done with the information? Has it changed, in some way, how they previously viewed God, prayer, or life? Or, after a period of time passing is it business as usual as though they never saw or heard what they did? Based on what I have seen and observed, both are true. Let's look at some examples of the Witnesses.

THE KNOWS AND THE NOS

I told my friend Brenda who I have known since college days and who my cousin Donne' called to come to the Emergency Room the night I was admitted that I was writing about some of the things related to my Testimony. She said "Oh…you have to tell them about the 'Knows' and the 'Nos'! Are you going to talk about that she asked me? Brenda has a way of looking at life events in simple terms. They are either black or white in her view, no matter how complex. I typically don't agree with her assessments because even when two situations appear the same, I will focus on those facts that make them different. Our perspectives are just different. Because of how Brenda sees the world, she summarized what occurred during my weeks in the ICU like this: "There were the Knows and the Nos."

Brenda told me that when she and Linda arrived at the Emergency Room, they were told that I was still being "worked on" meaning I had not yet been resuscitated and they continued to perform CPR. They were told that I may not make it through the night and if I did survive, I would likely be brain dead due to the amount of time I had been without a pulse. That was the first time, but not the last, that she would hear that prognosis and others similar to it. She travelled back and forth from Baltimore to the hospital various times during the 3 weeks that I spent in ICU hearing the reports, the conversations, seeing the tears, hearing the prayers and the songs. Not only did she hear things, but she also observed what people; the doctors, nurses, friends and family were doing. Even with all the activity, Brenda saw the events in the ICU in simple terms. Months after I had been released from the hospital while we were walking around the grounds of a campus where we had gone for a retreat, what Brenda said about the events in the ICU was that "there were two groups of people; the Knows and the Nos." By her assessment, the Knows were the people who know God and were praying because they believed that Jesus was able to heal me. The Knows were not letting what they saw in my lifeless body take over what they knew God could do. What they heard being said about my low chance of survival did not cause them to stop praying and trusting God. As for Brenda, she was part of the Knows group and told me that she never thought I would die. However, she thought my life would be very different with me not being able to live independently or doing things I previously had. She did not know how I would be, but she did not believe I was going to die. Brenda described the other group of people, the Nos, as those who said "no" I was not going to survive this or it was unlikely that I would make it through, or if I did make it, I would be brain damaged. The Nos looked only at what science was telling them about my condition and accepted that report. As my non-functioning kidneys started functioning, my internal bleeding stopped, I started squeezing hands, and responding to music and voices, Brenda said that she observed that some of those who were in the 'Nos' group became part of the 'Knows' group. The way Brenda saw things, although some of the 'Nos' started to believe that I would survive, it was because they were responding to the improvements they saw in my physical body, not because they genuinely believed in the power of God. For others in the original Nos group, she believed they did start to see that it had to be the power of God that was bringing me out because the science did not provide explanations for what was happening to me. Things did not make sense from a logical standpoint.

Throughout history, many people have said "No" to Jesus in part or in total for several reasons. But, somewhere along the way, some of those people have had an experience…an encounter…a revelation, that turned their No to a Know. Their switch was not a result of studying theology, but it was an undeniable encounter. Take the case of Apostle Paul in the Bible who at one point in his life, hated followers of Jesus Christ to such a degree that he was responsible for having many of them persecuted or killed. But, due to a life changing experience in which he encountered the power of Jesus[12], Apostle Paul went from being a chief persecutor of Christians to becoming a disciple of Jesus Christ, spreading the Gospel to many nations and being responsible for writing a majority of the New Testament!

When asked to provide a testimony about the goodness of God at her church's New Year Eve service when I was still in the hospital, but out of ICU and working towards being released, Brenda shared about what she called "her Christmas miracle". Her Christmas miracle that she talked about was how Jesus spared my life when all of the odds were against me. You see, Brenda had the right to claim my story as her testimony too because she prayed and was a witness to what happened. She also told the congregation about the 'Nos' and the 'Knows'. Brenda enjoys talking to people that she sits next to when travelling on an airplane. Inevitably, the conversation turns to her faith, and she may tell them about my miracle or other ways in which God has moved mightily in her life. At some point she says to them "Do you 'know' God? I know God! Let me tell you...I Know God!"

---

[12] Acts 9:1-19; Acts 22:6-21; and Acts 26:12-18.

> "All it takes is one move of God for a 'no' to turn into a 'know'."

CHOSEN TO REPRESENT: THE TWO COUSINS

Linda started calling people to inform them about my condition and my need for prayer the night I was admitted to the ER. In the first couple of days that I was in ICU, she wanted my pastor or someone else who was part of the church's leadership to come to the hospital and pray. Yes, she knew that people were already praying, but she wanted someone to come in person and pray over me. When Sheila, a friend and one of the Elders at my church, heard the news, she immediately told her family and our pastor so they could all pray. She told me months after I was released from the hospital that after the pastor, the next people she contacted were Michelle and Justin. Linda told me that she said to Sheila that "someone from the church has got to come here and pray!" It made sense that Linda would have called for the church leadership to come, but God had something else in mind.

Michelle told me that she and Justin were out having dinner when they received a call from Sheila telling them they needed to go to the hospital to pray for me. Michelle said that they looked at each other. One asked the other "What do we do?" It did not seem real. Everyone was out of town. They both knew that they had to go…go to the hospital that is, but there were questions. Some of the questions were voiced aloud and others were turning around in their heads. "Should it be us to go?" "We aren't part of the church leadership." "We haven't been ordained ministers!" "Should we be the ones from the church to go to ICU to pray for Charlma who is one of the ministers…one of the elders of the church?!"

Michelle

So, here they were, Michelle and Justin, in the car at night traveling the roads of DC having left their family to go to the hospital to see me. Michelle looked at Justin and said, "Are you ready for this?" Are you ready to go and pray for this woman of God who has prayed for us and others? Although she asked Justin, the question was for herself too. Months later Michelle would tell some of us at our worship gathering, through tears, how she felt conflicted knowing that she needed to go to the hospital to pray for me but at the same time telling God that she wasn't qualified...that this assignment should be for someone else to do. Her view of herself as not sufficient certainly wasn't unique as the Bible is full of those who were called by God to accomplish a purpose yet viewed themselves as not enough for the task. Take Moses for example, a man chosen by God to free Israel from captivity in Egypt under the reign of Pharaoh. He faced this assignment by asking God "Who am I that I should go to Pharaoh and bring the Israelites out of Egypt?" As though God had made a mistake in selecting him and wasn't aware of his strengths and weaknesses, Moses continued "O Lord, I'm not very good with words. I never have been, and I'm not now, even though you have spoken to me. I get tongue-tied, and my words get tangled."[13] One of the things the Bible says God told Moses was "Certainly I will be with you..."[14] As with Moses, so was God with Michelle and Justin. Even though Michelle was reasoning with God about why she was not qualified, she continued to move forward. Though she was conflicted some about why she was in the position of being one of the first people from my church to lay hands on me and pray, she was obedient and continued to this assignment that had been given her. That night was the first of many that she and Justin would come to my side.

Near the one-year anniversary of me being in the ICU, Michelle sent me a text message saying:

> *"Walking in, I didn't understand anything. Almost broke down, but the Holy Spirit rose up and said, 'not now, pray.' What God allows us to participate in for His glory, sometimes I don't get it, BUT I'm immensely grateful. I still say WOW!!"*

She hit the nail on the head, she, along with everyone else who was in the ICU and elsewhere who

---

[13] Exodus 4:10 (NLT).
[14] Exodus 3:12 (Amp).

prayed were allowed to participate in what God did; the miracle performed for His glory. That is "Wow!"

Justin

Justin told me that when they received the call to come to the hospital, he knew he and Michelle were to go, but he wasn't sure how he was to prepare to go. Should he take oil to anoint me? What should he do, he thought? Justin believed God was saying "Go…just go!" So along with Michelle, he arrived at the hospital. When he entered the ICU, walked across the room, and saw the condition I was in, he wondered what he was supposed to do. They prayed…indeed that is why they had come. He said he heard God saying that I was going to be all right and that "I was in there." Within the swollen, lifeless body in front of him, I was still "in there." Sometimes, people have a preplanned approach when they are going to pray for the sick. In other words, they go with an agenda that they have come up with before they arrive at their destination. In my case, Justin told me over dinner when we talked about his experience that "there was no strategy for what I saw in there. I couldn't have planned for it." Looking at the multiple tubes and pumps sustaining my body, God had let Justin know that I was fully in the body he was looking at. But as he stood with me, praying, he told me he heard the medical personnel mentioning something totally different. They were talking about 'thirty percent.' He wasn't sure whether they were saying I had a thirty percent chance of survival or that my brain function was only at thirty percent. Either way, the "thirty percent" report didn't make sense to Justin based on what he sensed God saying. He told me that during the first night in the ICU he asked himself "how can she be thirty percent if God said she is fully in there? If she is fully in there, that's it...she can't be thirty percent of anything." Also, if I was fully there and would recover, he wondered what was the purpose of him and his cousin being there; what were they to do?

    Justin told me that while he didn't have the whole picture, he knew that they were supposed to continue coming to the hospital to pray. Later, when the 24-hour prayer wheel was initiated at my church and everyone selected a one-hour time slot throughout the day and night to pray for me, Justin told me that he still felt he and Michelle were to physically be on site at the ICU and pray, so that is what they did. They were at the ICU that night and along with others continued to come and pray. He told me that there were times when some people were trying to stop the prayers and praise music going on in the ICU because they said it was disturbing me and causing my levels to rise. Justin said, "they were trying to quiet me down, but we were not going to stop praying!"

He said "It was fine if they did not want us praying in the room, we could go out in the hallway if they didn't want us in the ICU, but we were not going to stop praying! We were in the hallway praying!" I thank God that they did not stop! They knew why they were there.

A year after my miracle as Justin and I talked about that period when I was in the ICU and beyond, he said "It was an opportunity for us to witness the power of God and His authority. We thank God for what He did in your life and the hope of glory that it shows that we have in Him."

People do not need titles, positions, pedigrees, or special qualifications to be used by God! Anyone who is a follower of Jesus Christ just needs to say yes to whatever assignment is put before them, take steps forward, and let God do the rest. Michelle and Justin were available to represent my local church and pray in the room. By doing what they needed to do, they were blessed and expanded by God and have first-hand memories of God's power that they will never forget. They accepted their assignment and carried it out.

> *"God doesn't need people with titles to accomplish his purposes."*

GOD IS GOING TO FINISH THE WORK: The Outpouring Worship and Life Center (TOWLC)

Christians are told in Scripture that we are to walk by faith and not by sight. In other words, regardless of how situations look, we are to rely on the Word of God rather than being swayed by what we see, hear, and feel. One of the things that the Bible says is to pray; always pray. Feelings and emotions change but the Word of God does not, so we are taught not to be swayed by are feelings and emotions as they are fickle. Although we know this, when reality hits you in the face: death, loss, fear, loneliness etc., a person's faith can definitely be shaken! A vision of my body in the ICU would be that kind of situation for many which is why calls were made for people to come and see me since it was unlikely that I would make it. There were some who despite what they saw or heard, believed I would survive.

My pastor, Samuel Alan Burroughs and his wife, Merilyn Burroughs, were out of town visiting family when on Thanksgiving Day they heard the news of me being in ICU. Sheila, one of the ministers at my church and a dear friend, was also out of town when she was called about my situation; she contacted my pastor. My pastor told me that he and his family started praying right away as had Sheila, her husband Nate, and their family before she contacted him. By the time they all returned from their holiday travel, I had been in ICU for 5 days, was still on life support and in a medically induced coma. When they got back in town and came to the hospital, Pastor Burroughs recalls how dire my situation was: my swollen body almost not recognizable to him; the multiple tubes; and the talk going on about the need for dialysis and how I was not coming out of the coma. He told me that he did not want to hear anything about my medical condition but wanted to stay focused on his belief that God was going to bring me through the situation. He said that he knew that "this was not it for me; that I was not going to die because God was not finished with me." So, when people around him in the ICU talked about what was happening to me in medical terms or shared their predictions...he moved to another part of the room because he was not interested in what they were saying. He remained steadfast. He told me that he is typically very squeamish when it comes to seeing blood or seeing someone in a condition like I was in, but God strengthened him in such a way that he was not bothered. He had a strength and an assurance that he knew had to have come from God. He explained that he was so confident that I would recover that much of his time in the ICU was spent praying for others, the nurses, and their families. As we had dinner at a restaurant on Capitol Hill in Washington, DC a month after I left the hospital, I asked Pastor Burroughs and his wife Merilyn how they were able to believe God for my healing when they came to the ICU? By that time, I had seen a picture of myself with tubes everywhere and a listless stare. Merilyn said about her husband that "he really believed that God was going to bring you through, and I caught a hold of that and believed too!"

Some people may think "Sure, it is easy for them to say after the fact that they never doubted, but is that really true? After all, those 'religious people' always say things like that." I submit to any doubters that these statements were made by people who love and have a relationship with Jesus and whose faith was activated when there is no natural reason why it should have been! The evidence that I saw in text messages over a year after I was released from hospital supports that Pastor Alan and Elder Merilyn were full of faith believing that God would perform a miracle. The following are some examples:

Text from Merilyn to Church Family, November 22: *"Good evening TOWLC family: Please pray for Sis. Charlma. She is currently in ICU. Please join us in bombarding the throne on* *behalf of our sister. We trust God is in the room and performing the work!"*

Text from Merilyn to Church Family, November 23: *This text notified the church about a prayer call that night and ended with "Let's expect God to perform another miracle!"*

Video to Church Family from Pastor Burroughs, November 27: *This text notified the church about a prayer call that would be held on my behalf. During this call, 24 hours of prayer was instituted with members signing up for a one-hour period.*

Video to Church Family from Pastor Burroughs, November 25: *On the Monday after Thanksgiving, my Pastor provided an update after he and Merilyn had visited me. One of the things he said was that he was grateful for the privilege God gives us to bring things before Him. Despite my great improvement he asked that they continue to pray because my condition was still serious, and they should bear down even harder in prayer because the "the effectual fervent prayers the righteous avails much". He mentioned that when he shared with someone who was a nurse that the church was praying for me in shifts around the clock covering 24 hours and that the person responded that research showed that prayer was helpful and that he responded, "we didn't need research to tell us, we know it works and that God is faithful." He asked the church members to remain faithful in prayer believing that God is "able to do exceedingly abundantly above all we could ask or think." He stated further that God was going to do a complete work! "He is going to satisfy* her with long life, so we say yea and Amen to the plan of God."

Video to Church Family from Pastor Burroughs, November 29: *He shared that he had exciting news, that God was doing what He said He would do. He has felt the collective energy of their prayers. My kidneys were now fully functioning and fluid in heart and lungs had dissipated. Looking to remove breathing support etc. It was taking me awhile to come back. Because of the amount of time my brain was without oxygen the doctors were looking at options. He continued "But what we know is that God is not finished, He is going to do a complete work! So, I'm encouraging you to continue with effectual and passionate prayer. I'm inviting you to join me between, 5 and 9 in the morning; between 11 and 2 in the afternoon; and between 6 and 9 at night…I ask that you pray God will finish the work, I know He will. I am grateful that He has allowed us to partner with Him as He is performing this miracle." He stated that he was excited and looking forward to what God was going to do!*

I am so thankful for everyone at and connected to TOWLC that took the time to pray for me. It was not convenient for them. I will be forever grateful for the sacrifice!

> *"Praying should be our first choice, not our last resort."*

WARRIOR, GUARDIAN, AND COMFORTER

A year and a half after I had been released from the hospital, I spoke with Temaki , a friend and minister about my time in ICU and beyond. It wasn't the first time we had talked about that period; she had shared tidbits here and there, but on this day the conversation was different. Maybe it was because I had directly asked her on a few occasions for details. We scheduled and re-scheduled times to talk. I wanted to know about her involvement during that period beyond what I knew up to that point. Her name frequently came up; mentioned by friends and family members when they talked about my time in ICU. They were definitely impacted by her presence. One person sent a text during that period stating that my missionary sister Temaki came and changed their lives forever.

On a Saturday afternoon as we talked over the phone, Temaki began: "I woke up in the middle of the night with an intense urgency to pray." She continued "I stood up in the bed with my husband sleep next to me and I began to pray aloud in tongues. Then I started praying in English." She told me that she sensed a spirit of death threatening to, in her words, "take me out" so she was warring against this outcome through prayer! Indeed, the Warrior that she is was coming forth! Temaki was one of five people that I texted from the ER on November 21st simply telling them to pray. She heard nothing else from me that night, but the next day our friend and ministry partner Patrice contacted Temaki to tell her the severity of my condition and that I was in ICU.

Temaki told me that when she went to the ICU, she did not have a plan but knew that the Lord had told her to be there. She said that she felt assigned to be a protector, a keeper, a guardian in the spiritual realm knowing that death lurks around in hospitals. She said, "I knew my role was to speak life and provide spiritual food to your spirit." Temaki also felt that she was supposed to be a comfort to those who were there visiting me. She wanted to speak life and assure everyone that everything was going to be ok. She knew her assignment was different from some others. Yes, she prayed for me, and the decisions being made, but she was also praying for others and praying over the atmosphere in the ICU. Then, after some others left, she had to pray again because of the fear that they released in the room that needed to be cast out. She said, "I had to make sure you were covered!" Temaki told me God gave her the grace to do what she needed to do!

Temaki arrived at the hospital the day after she received the call about my condition. God was in control because people who ordinarily would not have been allowed to visit because they were not immediate family, were allowed to come in. As Temaki entered the isolated part of the ICU where I was, she approached me and said that my body looked lifeless. She was not affected by what she saw because "your spirit was strong within your body." Temaki did not want to alarm those who were in the room visiting but she prayed aloud; walking around the bed praying and touching my body: feet, arms, and head. At some point, she read the Bible aloud which she said she did for those in the room as well as to make sure that she was doing what needed to be done concerning me. Temaki then told me she started playing music (others have mentioned to me about the music she was playing)[15] and started singing. Temaki mentioned, as others have, that I reacted to the music. She said "you tried to get up out the bed. Your spirit was reacting to what was being played and you tried to take out the tubes." She felt certain that the worship

---

[15] One friend who was preparing to go to the hospital to give birth to her first child was putting together a list of songs she wanted to play while she was in labor. She contacted me and said she wanted the song that Temaki was playing at the hospital. I immediately knew which one it was because I remembered hearing the song as I laid in ICU unable to communicate but conscious of some things around me. I said to her, you're talking about "You Know my Name" by Tasha Cobbs and my friend said "Yes...that's it. I definitely want to add that song."

music had to continue as well as speaking the Word of God from the Bible over me.

She came to know that when she visited me in the hospital, she not only attended to me and saturated the atmosphere of the ICU with prayer and praise, but she was also to pray for, talk to, and comfort my friends and family who were there. She told me about a time when she was visiting along with another friend of mine who was sitting very quietly with tears in her eyes. Temaki said she told the young woman "I know she looks bad, but she is going to be alright." It is interesting that when my friends have mentioned other friends of mine that they met when visiting me and they describe them or tell me something about the person because they do not remember names, I typically know who it is that they are talking about. This situation that Temaki shared was no different; the few things she said about my friend who she comforted let me know who it was. When that woman and I had lunch after I got out of the hospital, she actually asked about Temaki and said that she definitely remembered her. In another conversation about a year later I shared with her the situation that Temaki told me about where she comforted someone crying. I told my friend that I thought it might have been her and she responded, yes, "I was having a hard time; it was me and I felt better after she talked to me."

Temaki carried out her assignment which included comforting others who were there to visit me.

> *"Knowing God's assignment for you in a given situation is critical."*

THE GIRLS

The 'girls' came. Linda, Janice, Kathy, Fay, Sheila, Sharon, Christy.[16] We've known each other since college and that is what we do; we come...we show up. They were concerned, scared even, not sure of what the outcome would be. But they were present...and they prayed! That is what we've always done through the decades, through thick and thin. We are there. They came alone and sometimes with their husbands[17] ;Linda, Janice, Kathy, Fay, and Sheila live in the Washington, DC area and came as though on assignment. Linda was the main disseminator of information and Janice one of my roommates in college and also after graduation was a registered nurse and kept abreast of what was being said from a medical standpoint. I heard that Janice read to me from the Bible though I was not conscious. Nonetheless, the Scripture fed me and stirred my

---

[16] We met in college as part of a sorority I used to be a member of, and within that larger group, there is a core group who have become my family...sisters...friends for life. Others from that core though not physically there, were "there" nonetheless. Like Kay who was praying or Jackie who was unable to visit due to a critical family situation, Michiko whose second granddaughter was about to be born, or Darla who prayed understanding that being in the geographic region where prayers are needed is totally unnecessary for God to hear and respond! Renee sent me a matching robe and house shoes (something I had never had) because she was insistent that I needed that. Every time I wear the robe, I reflect on the mercifulness of God. It is one of innumerable reminders!

[17] Fay's Kevin and Kathy's Michael.

spirit because one text message sent out to update people about my progress stated that I reacted by opening my eyes as Janice read to me. When my feeding tube was removed, I was restricted from eating and drinking because I had failed a 'swallow test.' I repeatedly begged for juice or water water...just a little because my mouth was so parched. The girls tried to assure me that I would soon be able to get something to drink, but "not quite yet" they said; "In a little while", "pretty soon" they told me. I heard them talking about a test I had failed. Kathy finally could not take me begging for drink in my barely audible voice anymore and one night, she put some juice on a sponged swab and put it to my lips. Wow! It was refreshing; so very refreshing. It made me want more, but that would be all I would get until I left the ICU. Sharon and Christy came on the train from New Jersey and Philadelphia to see me and talk to me but when I was in ICU, I did not know they were there. Talking about her visit a couple of years after I left the hospital, Christy talked about how bad I looked; I was still on life support when she came to visit and sat by my bed. She said that my friend Elaine, who Christy knew from our college days because the three of us danced in the college's dance company, came and sat next to her and told her that I wasn't going to make it. Christy told me she did not want to hear that I wasn't going to make it and that she told Elaine

"God has the final say". The two of them sat staring at a picture that Christy brought of the three of us in a dance position.

Once I was out of ICU, hardly a day went by that one of the girls was not there rubbing my head, massaging my feet, sitting with me, encouraging me, loving me. They are all witnesses. Linda was the gatekeeper, coming to visit me every day and I've been told that she refused to leave my side some days in ICU because she wanted to hear what the medical staff were saying. One of my friends from work said about Linda "she is who you want on your side!" During one of my visits with Sheila after I was in my patient room, I teased her saying that she and 'the girls' were like my caseworkers because they were there to do whatever I needed. Sheila is a woman of faith, who has relied upon the mercies and promises of God in many situations. After I left the hospital Fay gave me tips about strengthening exercises I needed to do. At a celebratory gathering some of us had at Kathy and Michael's house a month after I was released from the hospital, Fay told me when we had a moment alone in the dining room, "they told us that you wouldn't be able to live on your own...that you would probably need to be in an assisted living situation. We said, well, if that is what was needed, well that's just what it was." The message I took away from Fay telling me that was if my life was going to be totally different than it had been before, and if I would need help to that degree; so be it! They would still be there for me.

> *Love is an action word.*

UP FROM ALABAMA

When Patrice arrived at the ICU on the Sunday after I was admitted in the ICU, she and her husband Frank had only been home a day or two after having driven almost eight hundred miles to their home in Virginia from Alabama where some of their family members had been in a horrible accident leaving them in critical condition. Patrice, a minister, and mighty prayer warrior who prays with focus and authority, was one of the key people I texted from the ER when I first arrived asking for prayer. She later heard more details about what happened to me from a text sent by my friend, who attended my church. Had Patrice not heard from him, I don't know how long it would have taken for her to receive word. So much would have been different in terms of the timing of the prayer that went out across nations on my behalf. It was not a coincidence that Patrice and my friend met. I had introduced them only about 6 months earlier because of similarities in their ministries and because I really felt they and their spouses should connect and fellowship. Although Patrice and Marcus and their spouses never had the opportunity to meet face to face, it was Marcus who let Patrice know about my situation while she and Frank were still in Alabama. Patrice told me that when Marcus called her, he told her talking about me, "Sis, she actually left us for 25 minutes." After hearing this, I'm sure it made sense to her that she had not heard from me since the night of November 21st when I sent the text saying, "Pray in ER."

Patrice and Frank were already in the midst of a crisis situation with their family in Alabama when she received the call, but they began interceding in prayer for me. With everything happening with their family and then with me, Patrice shared with me when I talked to her in preparation for this book that she was feeling pretty overwhelmed at the time and was not sure her prayers would be effective, but she nonetheless started praying for me anyway. That's what prayer warriors do; they press through regardless of how they 'feel' knowing that feelings are temporary and are not what should dictate the actions of followers of Jesus Christ. Indeed, the Bible says that God's strength is made perfect in our weakness! [18] Patrice also contacted Dr. Clarke, one of my mentors in ministry and friend, and Temaki, a sister in the ministry, to tell them of my condition. Temaki, Patrice and I formed a very special bond since meeting and ministering together on a mission trip Dr. Clarke led in West Africa 12 years ago. Since then, we have remained friends and supported each other in

---

[18] II Corinthians 12:9, Apostle Paul sharing a revelation he received from Jesus.

ministry and life. Patrice contacting Dr. Clarke and Temaki resulted in prayer going forth for me in Africa, Asia, the Middle East, and Europe.

Patrice told me that when she arrived on her first visit to the ICU, a friend who had been sitting with me had to leave, which left Patrice by herself with me, which was perfect. As I laid there with tubes everywhere, eyes closed, and machines beeping she said she began praying over me and playing some worship music of a woman that she recalled me telling her some years prior that I really liked. As bad as I looked, she told me that she never felt hopeless or that I was not going to make it. She said "God had already shown Himself faithful…He had already performed the miracle. When you coded, He didn't have to bring you out, but He did." What the miracle did for her at that point was assure her that God had moved on my behalf, and I would survive. Her husband Frank confirmed what she believed on one of the visits when he came as she recalls him saying "Charlma is going to be alright." Only God can enable someone to speak life in the face of death.

Patrice was not just a friend who came to visit, but she was one of a core group of people specifically assigned to pray for me just like a soldier is assigned to a particular post in the military. In the month and a half that I was in the hospital, she would travel from Fredericksburg, VA to DC every week to see me, sometimes with her husband but typically alone. They of course prayed often at home too. Just like others who understood the power of prayer and the importance of being led by Holy Spirit, I was not the only person she prayed for when she came if she was led to pray for others. Also, like at least two others who came to pray for me, Patrice paid attention to what was being said about me in the ICU; she was on guard. Patrice told me about a time when she was visiting me, and someone said that I was going to need to have a trach inserted. She said that she immediately started praying and making declarations that opposed that statement because she believed God had already healed me whether I looked like it or not. She told me that her speaking in opposition to that diagnosis was not a personal affront against the person who made the statement, but she said she could not just let those words go unchecked. Instead, she spoke words of healing and victory in the situation. Patrice took authority over the atmosphere in the ICU by declaring words, in the Name of Jesus, that did not match up with the body (mine), that was before her.

    Patrice told me that during another visit her intent was to read scriptures aloud over me, however, when she took out her Bible to get started, one of the nurses asked her to leave for a little while as they needed to attend to me.

THE MIRACLE, THE WITNESSES AND ME

Initially she was disappointed about this, but when Patrice went out in the hall, she encountered a woman from another country whose husband had been hit by a car. The woman did not know anyone in DC and was visibly shaken. Patrice sat with the lady, prayed for her, and tried to encourage her. She even gave the lady her phone number in case she needed anything since she didn't know anyone in the area. The woman appeared relieved and much calmer. By the time the nurse came to get Patrice so she could come back into the room, visiting hours were over. On that day, God used Patrice to help someone other than me so her purpose for making the trip was still accomplished, it was just a different purpose than she thought when she headed up Interstate 95 to DC on that day! The fact that she was open and available to be used in a way contrary to her original plan, enabled her to be used by God to help someone else in need. If Patrice had left the hospital because she was asked to leave my room, she would not have been in position to carry out her special assignment for that day.

> *"God uses yielded vessels to carry out his purposes."*

I'M GOING TO TAKE YOUR RED BOOTS!

I am known to wear cowboy boots. My friend Rick came to visit me in ICU and like many others tried to get a reaction out of me during a period when the medical personnel considered me non-responsive. During one of his visits, Rick told me that if I did not wake up, he was going to take my red cowboy boots. When he said those words, he and others who were in the ICU saw me move my foot. It's interesting because I recall hearing someone say something about my boots, and I specifically remember moving my foot. I just did not know who it was talking to me.

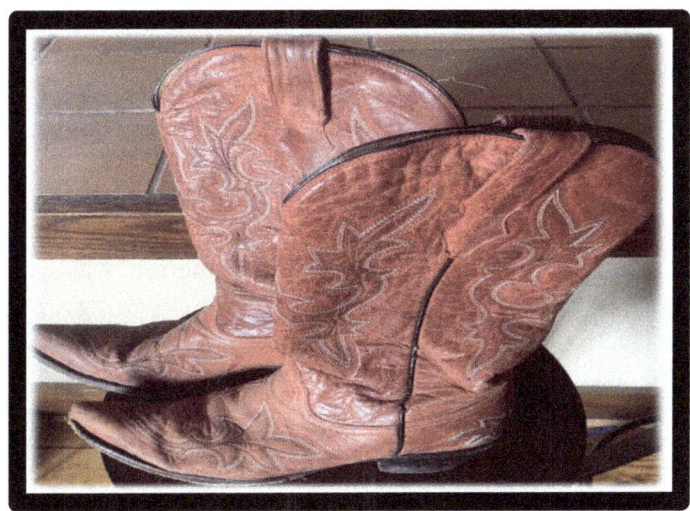

YOU WERE IN THERE

"I knew you were in there"! Several of the witnesses including my pastor have made this comment to me, or one similar to it. The comment is a declaration in opposition to what the medical personnel told them when I was in ICU; when I was not responding, and they deemed there was nothing else they could do for me. These people, some of the witnesses that is, believed that even in my broken state, I was hearing, I was understanding, I was resting, or I was communing with God.

The doctors, of course, wanted me to improve but in the days following my resuscitation, I was not making significant progress. They sought stimuli that I would react to…familiar voices…music etc. So, lots of people were beckoned to come or call and talk to me hoping that one voice would be the special key to unlock something within me. The thing is, sometimes I did respond by the nod of my head when certain music was played, or scripture read. Three people even shared with me about a time when someone was reading scripture and I tried to get up off the bed. They considered my actions a response to the word of God. But, for the most part, I was not responding from a medical perspective, and definitely not with any consistency. At one point I was a mere two days from being taken off of life support because I was not improving. My friend Elaine told me that during this period, she whispered in my ear emphatically saying, "Charlma, girl you better do something and wake up because they're about to take you off of life support!" I have no recollection of her pleading.

Although I was not responding on que to the people around me, I periodically recognized voices and knew things happening. Two voices I recall hearing during my 'non-responsive' period were those of Sheila Edmonds and her daughter Shamika. They had come with Nate, Sheila's husband. Shamika has the sweetest voice and I always love how she uniquely says my name. My eyes were not open, but I heard her say in an upbeat way "Hi Sister Charlma." Just like I clearly remember her greeting me, I also remember that I did not respond. I don't know if it was because I physically couldn't because I was still on a ventilator or maybe my mind just couldn't figure out how to make that happen. I have no idea. Shamika was surprised when I told her years after that visit that I heard her because there was nothing from my outward appearance that would indicate that. By contrast to Shamika's expression, I heard the sadness in her mother's voice when she called my name. She very slowly said "Sister Charlma" drawing out those words. I know seeing me like that was hard. The way Sheila said my name was as if to say, 'come on sis...wake up!' Again...I didn't respond, but I heard.

My friend Janice told me that she and others knew I was "in there" because I would respond to certain things. She told me that on one occasion, she shared with one of the nurses on duty that I had responded by moving my hand, but the nurse did not believe her. The nurse told Janice that she just 'thought' she saw me respond, but I really had not. Apparently, that happens sometimes when friends and family project what they want to see their loved ones doing. However, Janice was sure that I had responded. She is a seasoned registered nurse and is familiar with those situations where a family member imagines that a loved one is responding because they want it so badly, but Janice knew what she saw me do and was encouraged by it. Another friend, Cecily, told me that during a visit when she visited me in the ICU, before she left she leaned in and told me that she would be back to see me but that she and her mother, who was with her at the hospital, were going to see Michelle Obama talk about her new book. She said she told me that she knew I would understand. Cecily said I put my hand up for her to hold and she did. While I don't remember what she told me, I do remember lifting my hand up for someone to hold. I mention elsewhere in this book about how a friend told me he was going to take my red cowboy boots if I did not wake up and how he and others saw me move my foot. I recall moving my foot. There were other accounts of people witnessing me react to things.

Despite my medical failures, like not passing a swallow test that would have allowed me to not be dependent on tube feeding, the periodic reactions from me were enough to convince and stoke the confidence of some and confirm what others believed they heard God saying about my future; that this was not the end of my story. Some knew that, yes, I was "still in there!"

> *"With God, there is always more than Meets the eye."*

A MIRACLE WITNESSING A MIRACLE

Laying in the bed, still in ICU, I was moving back and forth between states of consciousness, dreaming[19], and seeing and hearing bits and pieces of the activity going on around me. Consequently, after my release from the hospital I would talk about something that happened when I was in ICU and some people would be surprised that I remembered it because I looked so 'out of it' or they had been told by the medical staff that I was not responsive. For example, I learned of the death of a friend's mother during this period when I heard some of my friends talking about it among themselves as they were by my bed. I remember thinking to myself that they had gotten the facts mixed up, but in any case, I heard the discussion and it registered. There was one very memorable encounter that I recalled from this period that I am so happy occurred exactly as I remembered.

One night, as I lay in bed, I had a visit from Khaliah and her husband, Dee Jay; a visit I will never forget. Khaliah had specifically come to tell me about a miracle involving them. I like to call this visit a miracle, witnessing a miracle because at this point, I was a miracle! Having moved from

---

[19] See the Chapter on "Dreams".

being dead without a pulse for 26 minutes, then to life support for 12 days, to being alive and off of life support. I was still in ICU...and not out of the woods from a medical perspective. The doctors wouldn't find out until later, I had absolutely no brain damage; no broken bones, despite the continuous pounding on my chest for 26 minutes by the fantastic CPR professional on duty! So, I was a miracle at this point!

I remember my friend's bright smile as she was at the foot of my bed; the whole room seemed bright to me though I don't know whether it really was. I remember Khaliah being so happy. As she smiled from ear to ear, she said "Charlma, hi!" I responded "Hi" in an extremely low voice. She continued, "We had to come by to tell you, you're one of our angels...you've been praying...we're going to have a baby! We're pregnant. We both are!"[20] I was sooooooooo happy. I smiled or, at least I tried to smile. I recall saying "Thank You Jesus!" ..., though I don't know if it was audible. She told me her husband was there and he approached the foot of the bed so I could see him and was also smiling. This was so incredibly special to me because I had been praying about this couple having a baby for a couple of years. She and I had talked about their great

---

[20] I found out some time later that when Khaliah said, "we both are", she was referring to her and her sister who was also expecting a baby.

difficulties trying to conceive. They were praying and trusting God through the process, but it was a very stressful situation. I would always try to encourage her, but I knew how very hard the journey had been. In fact, the doctor gave them little, if any, hope that they would be able to conceive a child. They said the likelihood that it would happen on their own was very small; like…virtually no chance. At the time of this particular visit, my friend was about three and a half months pregnant. Of course, she had a smile big enough to light up the room and of course she felt it was very important to make a special trip to tell me the news.

Khaliah told me months after I was released from the hospital that she was determined to come tell me. She had been advised not to come; I was in the ICU after all, and she was pregnant. She was also advised to check with one of my friends who was providing my updated status to people to make sure it was ok to come, but Khaliah told me she had decided she wasn't going to check with anyone! Clearly, she was determined, and she trusted God to take care of the details! It was as if the environment at the hospital that night was set up perfectly for her to share her good news because she told me that even though the ICU typically had a lot of people there to visit me, she and her husband were the only ones there when they came. She told me that she was not sure whether they would be allowed to come in and that she was shocked when they entered and no one else was there. They had not shared the news with many people at this point, so she really wanted privacy and that is exactly what they got! Again, God was all in the process.

After they left, I went into a dream that continued seamlessly from their visit. It seemed to go on for a long time. Later, when I was in my patient room, I wondered at one point whether the news shared with me was real. Could it have been a dream? No, I knew the part about the baby was not a dream! But just to make sure, the first time I talked to Khaliah after that visit was when she called my hospital room. I asked her "Khaliah, did you tell me something when you came to visit me?" She simply said, "Yes." Though she couldn't see me through the phone, I was ecstatic.

God brought life to two dead situations. He restored me and brought forth my Khaliah and DJ's beautiful daughter, Nasirah.[21]

Jesus is still a miracle worker.

---

[21] The couple was also blessed with a second beautiful daughter, Zoe born in 2021. God always has the final say!

SOLDIERS

One visit from two colleagues from my current workplace is significant for two reasons. First, although I was still in ICU, I clearly remember them being there. This was not typical for me during this period in ICU because although I remember some visits or portions of them, I was unaware of most of the visits. Through the years, different people have said they visited me…or prayed over me…or that so and so person sang to me, but I had no knowledge that these events were happening. Second, I was very encouraged by their visit, but some of the things I found so encouraging did not actually happen, but rather occurred in a dream I had while they were visiting me. In other words, I was encouraged by some things they actually did, and I was also encouraged by some things I dreamt they did. Let me explain.

I was no longer on a ventilator when they came and had significantly improved but I still was not well enough to be moved out of the critical care unit. My eyes were closed while they were there, yet I was aware of their presence and recognized their voices. I remember thinking how nice it was that they had come. One of them shared with me that not too many years before, he had been in a similar position, and he got better and expected me to get better too. I can still hear the tone of his voice. I was touched by what he shared, and a tear rolled down my cheek. I remember that exchange and both of them confirmed that it happened when I talked to them 3 years after leaving the hospital. I mention that they 'confirmed' the exchange because during my period in the ICU, reality sometimes collided with my dreams. Their visit was a prime example because not everything I recalled really happened. For example, it seemed to me that they were walking back and forth around my bed, similar to soldiers and praying. In fact, I heard them saying the Lord's Prayer" Our Father, Who Art in Heaven, Hallowed be Thy Name…" I also heard one of them saying the name of Jesus. I really appreciated them being there and praying for me. However, I recall being confused that they would say that prayer because one of them was not a Christian. I remembered thinking, "He is Jewish, why would he be saying the Lord's prayer?" I knew that the Lord's prayer was not part of his religious tradition. Well…the reality is… he wasn't saying that prayer; I was dreaming. When I mentioned to him what I remembered about the two of them praying, he assured me that, yes, he had held my hand and tried to encourage me by telling me his story and how deeply touched he was by that exchange, but he was clear that he was not praying. He said he would never pray in an environment like that. He told me that maybe it was my other colleague who was praying as that was something he might do. When I asked my other colleague, he replied without hesitation "Oh...I was definitely praying...yes, I was praying for sure; but not aloud." I was praying silently. So, what I thought had occurred, in the way I thought it had occurred, had not.

The visit from my colleagues demonstrated to me that amazingly, even when I had dreams during this period, God was strengthening me in them through prayers, scriptures, and words of encouragement.[22] How wonderful that was.

> *"You never know who God will use to bless your life; expect the unexpected!"*

---

[22] See, the chapter on "Let the Children Come" where I discuss a dream, I had about my Godson Amir giving me words of encouragement.

THEY SAW FOR THEMSELVES

Sometimes it is just not enough to hear about an event second-hand; even if the description of the event is told by people you trust. I understand this as I am the type of person who likes to see, hear, and experience things for myself rather than relying on what someone else says about it. I believe many people are like that. The growth of Jesus' ministry is a prime example of this mindset in people where they wanted to see things for themselves.

As Jesus went from place-to-place performing miracles, the word of His mighty acts spread quickly because those who witnessed the miracles told others who then told others who then told others to the point that crowds followed Jesus so they could see for themselves what was going on. In my situation too, there were those who had seen me at my worst and who came back, to see for themselves what was going on with me; I share a few of those encounters.

The Doctor - He moved slowly around the corner...

I'll never forget an encounter I had with a doctor who visited me. It was a sunny day in December after I had been transferred out of ICU to a step-down floor and I was at a point where I could sit upright in a chair if someone could get me to the chair. I was so happy to be able to look out of the window to see how the weather was. I sat there patiently waiting for whatever would come next be it lunch, a check-in by a nurse or a visit from a friend. As the doctor entered my room, I looked towards him with an expectant look on my face. Was he going to explain something about my condition or check my vitals? It certainly was not unusual that a doctor would come to my room; I lost count of the doctors coming in and out. But there was something a little strange. The first thing that was unusual was the way the doctor entered my room. He did not enter with the brisk, confident stride and authoritative expression of most of the physicians. Instead, this doctor came in with slow, cautious, tentative steps. The next thing was that as he moved towards me, he stared at me with a startled look. He did not take his eyes off me as though he wanted to make sure I was who he thought I was. Still staring, this doctor slowly told me his name saying, "I'm Dr. _____ I saw you in ICU." I responded, "nice to meet you." You have to understand that him saying that he saw me in ICU did not really fill in any dots for me. There were no thoughts in my head like "Ah, he saw me when I was in a coma!" or "He knows how bad off I was." Yes, I knew I had been in ICU, but not many other details. At this point, neither my family, friends, nor doctors had told me the extent of my condition in ICU because not knowing what all led me to the state I had been in, they did not want to cause any stress for fear that it might negatively impact me. They had no idea that God had already done the healing work. So, I did not comprehend why this doctor was acting strangely. I had no idea that it was hard for him to believe I was the same person he had seen in ICU; the one not expected to survive. He then said, "I heard about you...they told me, and came to see..." then his voice drifted off as he extended his hand. I shook his hand and told him again that it was nice to meet him as he continued to look like he was in shock. In front of him was the same person he had seen lifeless...unable to swallow...unable to breath on her own...unable to respond...but now was sitting up in a chair, mentally cognizant, alert, saying "nice to meet you." The difference between him and most of the other doctors was that while the others depended on the notes in my chart to get information about what my condition had been, this doctor had seen, firsthand, in the ER and ICU. He saw as it took 26 minutes to get my heart started. He saw that I remained non-responsive for longer than the medical staff felt comfortable with to the point of them saying there was nothing else they could do and recommending that I be taken off life support. The impact was greater for him. That is why he entered the room so slowly not knowing what he would see on the other side of the wall and, once he saw, he was lost for words.

He then turned and left the room, perhaps not knowing he had witnessed a person who had been touched by the power of God but at least knowing for sure that what he had just seen was beyond his understanding. I wonder what thoughts went through his mind. I don't remember him saying bye. The doctor heard...he came...and he saw! He saw for himself. I'll venture to say that he will not forget the encounter.

Amanda - She quietly watched and saw for herself...

Amanda saw me when I was in ICU...unconscious...in really bad shape. I remember a very special visit when she came back to see me after I had been moved out of ICU to a 'step down' patient room. She had probably heard I was doing better but she took the long journey into DC from one of the further out suburbs of Maryland to visit me; to see me for herself. It was before Christmas and with two young children, I'm sure she had many things she needed to do. Amanda came in my room with craft paint and Christmas tree decorations that she painted as she sat by my bed. It thrilled me to see her painting the decorations for me! So sweet. I recall her saying shortly after she arrived that I looked so much better, but she did not go into details about how I was before and how I was now.

She just sat down near the foot of my bed, painting and periodically looking up at me. I noticed her observing me, but again, she was calm. When my food was brought in, she asked what I needed help with, and she continued to quietly observe. I likely asked her to open the top on the protein drink I had every day because at that point, I did not have enough strength to open those bottles. She left the ornaments that she painted for me and left.

A couple of weeks later Amanda came back, this time with my friend Merilyn, my pastor's wife and a leader from my church who was one of the initial people I had asked to pray for me when I first arrived at the ER on November 21st. It was another nice visit. Merilyn commented on my improvement since she had last seen me. Again, my lunch came during the visit and I proceeded to cut the chicken in front of me which was a surprise to Merilyn because she knew I was a vegetarian. Amanda commented about how much I had improved even since her visit a couple of weeks prior. She said, "Even the way you are using the utensils to feed yourself has improved so much!" She sounded happy. I knew that Amanda had to go to work, and I was a little concerned that she and Merilyn had stayed too long and that she might be late for work. After they left, I sent a text message to Merilyn and asked whether Amanda was on time for work. She told me that she was on time and then said, "She kept saying as we left the hospital, 'I'm amazed at what God has done!'"

Yes... Amanda had come, and come again, and saw for herself what God had done!

Rick - He came with flowers

Rick also had visited when I was in ICU during a period when the medical staff wanted me to hear familiar voices that would cause a reaction from me and return me to consciousness. He is the person who told me during that visit that if I didn't wake up that he would take my red cowboy boots. He thought that would rile me for sure since my affinity for cowboy boots was well known. Though he as well as other friends around my bed at that time saw me move my foot when he made that statement, the medical staff did not see it, nor did they trust that it had really happened. And, if it had happened, the subtle reaction of me moving my foot was not what they were looking for as a marker to assess my progress.

One evening in late December after I had left ICU and was in a room where I was closely monitored yet definitely not to the degree I had been in ICU; Rick came again to visit me. He brought beautiful flowers for me from him and his wife. I was so happy to see him. There were others visiting me when he came and we all talked and laughed. At one point after I said something, I saw him looking at me and slightly nodding his head up and down as he smiled with a satisfied look. He left shortly thereafter explaining he needed to pick up some things for dinner for he and his wife.

I reflected upon that visit at different times after leaving the hospital, especially how Rick had nodded his head and smiled before leaving. It wasn't until a few years after I left the hospital and was talking to Shaquana, a mutual friend who considers herself Rick's 'play sister', about the period when I was non-responsive in ICU that Rick's reaction during that visit made sense. She told me about how she was praying for me and had so many other people praying for me as well. She asked Rick to hold the phone to my ear when he visited as she prayed and pleaded with me to wake up. Then she said, "I know a lot of people were praying for you to survive, but I was praying not only that you would survive, but that you would be in your right mind, like you were before and do the things you used to do. I did not want you to just be alive." When she said that, something clicked for me as my mind went back to my hospital room when Rick visited me. I recalled his satisfied expression back then and how he slightly nodded his head when I was engaging in conversation and laughing. It now made perfect sense to me. In the ICU he previously had seen me hooked up to tubes and laying with a dazed expression, not responding. I imagine that when he heard I was better and was no longer in ICU he was thankful, but he likely did not want to rely on what he was hearing. Instead, he came to see me for himself. So, during his visit on that evening when he saw me talking and joking around with him and the others, he seemed satisfied with what he was seeing. As he looked at me and nodded his head, it was as if he was saying 'yeah…she's going to be fine…she sounds like herself. She's good…I'm good.'

Just like the doctor and Amanda, Rick came to see for himself. Sometimes we need to do that; instead of taking someone else's word about a situation, we need to see for ourselves.

> *"Seek out what God is doing for yourself."*

WHAT WILL HAPPEN TO CHARLMA?

My friend Janice told me that one evening when my Aunt Charlye was visiting me at the hospital, as she sat there, she said out loud "What is going to happen to Charlma?" It was obvious that the gravity of my situation, highlighted by the grim reports of the medical staff had her concerned. She was probably thinking about the fact that I lived alone, in West Virginia, fifty miles outside of DC and if I would not be able to take care of myself, what would happen? Where would I go? Janice said my aunt then said that my Godbrother Eric said he would take me back to Toledo, Ohio (my birthplace) and care for me. My aunt then concluded by saying "we are in agreement with that."

Eric had been looking out for me since I was three years old coming to my 'rescue' at nursery school when a little boy was trying to play with me. Imagine that! Some child, other than him, had the nerve to play with me. Eric approached the little boy and made it clear that no one was to play with me but him. His protective nature concerning me continued from that point through the years. Before my mother died, she asked him to look out for me and he took her request seriously. Very seriously! Therefore, for him to step up and plan to relocate me back to Toledo to care for me once I got out of the hospital; if, I got out of the hospital, made sense and as my aunt said, my family agreed with that.

On the night I went to the ICU, Eric told me that Elaine called him around midnight to let him know what was going on with me and explain that I might not make it through the night. By this time, my heart had stopped for 26 minutes, and I had been resuscitated but remained in a very fragile state. After receiving the call, praying with his family who he was celebrating Thanksgiving with, and contacting his Godson to pray for me, he started preparing to come to DC. After I had made it through the night, Eric flew into DC arriving at the hospital the day after I had been admitted.

Eric is a man of action and after seeing me and hearing the grave prognosis, on this first trip to DC, he began to think about what practical things would need to be done for me. At some point during the first week that he was in DC, he, and my cousin Donne' went to my apartment to look for important information, talk to my landlord, and start the process of taking care of my affairs. However, God had another plan that was completely different from what they thought would be needed. There were miracles in the works!

God's ways are not like our ways.

LET THE CHILDREN COME

"Let the children come to me, and don't try to stop them. People who are like these children belong to God's kingdom." Matthew 19:14

I have always had a special place in my heart for children and young people. From the time of my first babysitting job at 12 and working at a Daycare at 14 to being blessed with amazing Godchildren, many God-given nieces, nephews, as well as "sons" and "daughters" in the nations where I have ministered. So, it is totally understandable; expected really, that children and young people would be included among the number of witnesses. When certain traumatic events occur, we adults often leave children out of the process because we want to shield them...protect them from the trauma. We don't want them exposed to information or situations that are beyond their maturity level. However, in trying to shield them, we can sometimes prevent them from gaining valuable life experiences. As recorded in the book of Matthew, Jesus demonstrated for us the importance of including children. Jesus told His disciples not to stop the children from approaching Him and proceeded to tell the disciples that they needed to have faith like the children had. The little children needed to see the miracles and hear the teachings of Jesus just as the adults did. They needed to be right in the mix and Jesus wanted them there. In the account of Jesus feeding 5,000 with a couple of fish and a few loaves of bread, that account in the Book of John reports that this scant amount of food that Jesus multiplied, came from the lunch of a little boy who along with the multitude of the grown men and women was also in attendance to be taught by Jesus. I mention this just to highlight that children have something to offer and should not be disregarded. In my situation, there were children who prayed for me, made get-well cards, and in one instance visited me when I left ICU. Teenagers were also involved in my miracle. My Godson Amir visited me in the ICU; he was the only underaged person allowed to come in. He came again when I was in my hospital room. Maggie, who I have known since birth and am an 'aunt' to due to my relationship with her mother Sharon knew I was ill and visited me once I left ICU. Also, Terri from my church who I've known since she was a toddler came to visit me in my hospital room with her mother and one of her aunts. What joy these visits were for me. For these children and teenagers, seeds of faith were planted whether they realize it or not, and perhaps years from now when they are going through a difficult time or situation that appears impossible, they will remember what God did for me.

I received songs and prayers recorded by young girls in a village in northern Ghana who were interceding for me. Closer to home, I received an energetic video message from the three children of Tim and Erika Lewis who along with their parents attended my church. In the video, from the back seat of their parents' car, they told me in unison that they hoped I felt better and expressed their love. While at the time they did the video, I was not aware of it, when I looked at it two years later, I was so humbled...felt so much gratitude. These children saw me months after making the video walk into church and participate in our worship service as I had prior to going into the hospital. My prayer is that at some point in their lives, they will remember the before and after of my ordeal. I received another special treat when the daughter of another young couple from my church asked if she could come see me because she wanted to give me a picture she had drawn. There had been restrictions on children that young coming to my room, but late one night (quite late) about two and a half weeks before I was released from the hospital, little Simone came with her parents to see me and deliver her picture. I was thrilled! Looking back, I believe her father knew it was important for them to come and was keenly aware that moments like these should not be taken for granted. After being in my room for a few minutes,

Simone said to her parents "can I hug her?" That was the best hug; I needed it.

When I was still in a coma and not responding, I was told that the doctors became increasingly concerned and said that people whose voices I would definitely recognize and react to needed to come to hopefully bring me out of the coma. As an aside, my pastor later told me that he knew it wasn't necessary for a familiar voice to stimulate me because Jesus could bring me out of the coma on his own, or I could respond to an unfamiliar voice such as the voice of one of the nurses or someone emptying the trash in the room. But, not factoring God into the equation, the medical staff wanted a familiar voice. My cousin said the doctor asked who was someone that I really loved and would respond to and that they all responded "Amir." Amir, my Godson was the person who they figured could wake me if anyone could. Several people who were there when he visited told me later how rough it was for him to see me in the condition, I was in. A couple of them talked to him. I did not come out of the coma during that visit from Amir. However, I believe that Amir needed to see me so the experience could be marked within him. My prayer is that it will serve him well in the future. He will be able to testify that God made a way out of no way. Although I did not wake up during that visit, I had a dream about Amir coming to see me and God spoke to me through the dream. In the dream, Amir leaned in close to me, almost face to face and said in a low voice in my ear "This isn't too much to get through, is it?" Though it was a question, it was being said as though it was a statement...as though he was telling me that my situation was not too much for me to get through. In the dream, I was quiet and Kathy, Amir's other Godmother said "Charlma, Amir is talking to you." He then repeated his question, and I shook my head back and forth. I said "No, it is not too hard." After getting out of the hospital, I asked Amir and Kathy about the situation and both of them told me that it had not happened. That is when I realized that it was a dream. Even though I did not respond to Amir during that visit, I knew he was there, which led to the dream I had. At any rate, God used Amir to encourage me in another realm, which was as real to me as the one that everyone else was experiencing.

Let the children come; don't stop them. Their presence is powerful and should not be trivialized. Children are used by God to accomplish His purposes. In my situation, I am confident that the prayers of the children were heard.

> *"Children are used by God too; don't underestimate them."*

WERE ANGELS THERE?

One of the things my Godbrother Eric has mentioned on several occasions about his time visiting me in the ICU, is the visit from my close friend Tom who used to attend my church. Eric told me that on one occasion people were praying for me and that Tom walked in and said something about Angels. Eric was not sure whether he said, "I see Angels" or "the Angels are here," but all he knew was that Tom mentioned Angels. Eric has had more than one experience in his life where he believed that he had been assisted by the intervention of Angels, so when he heard Tom mention Angels, Eric was not shocked or taken aback but it got his attention. He accepted as true that there might be ministering angels in the room. Eric told me that one of our friends who was also there started questioning about where the angels were. He said that he told her that she would not be able to see them, and he suggested that they leave and go to the cafeteria to get a bite to eat so that Tom and others who were there would have the freedom to pray as they wanted. I of course had to validate this account, not because I doubted Eric because I didn't, but I wanted to hear what Tom had to say. I asked Tom about it on a couple of occasions, and he told me that he did not recall specifically what he said when he walked into the room where I laid, but since he has never seen angels, he would not have said that he saw them. What he did know was that when he entered the ICU area, he sensed a strong angelic presence. He was sure of that.

SHE GOT DOWN ON HER KNEES

One day after I had been out of the hospital for four months, I was catching a ride with my friend Genell going to her house to celebrate the law school graduation of her eldest daughter Neah. Not too long after we pulled out of the parking lot and sat in the long line of cars trying to leave the law school campus, she turned to me and said, "I can tell you this now; I'm just going to let it out." She went on to tell me that during a visit when she and Neah had come to visit me that I really did not look as though I was going to make it. She said that I looked like I was on my way home to be with Jesus. Genell continued, "I knew that I could not leave that room without praying for you, but I just couldn't; I didn't have it in me. It was too hard." So, she turned to her daughter and said to her "Neah, you pray." She told me that without hesitation, Neah got right down on her knees… on the floor in the ICU and started praying!!! Whew! Hallelujah! As I write this now and reflect on that conversation and picture the earnest prayer of faith that went out through Neah as she kneeled in the ICU, I can feel the power that was released! I am so very thankful! I am thankful that Neah, someone whose diaper I had changed when she was a baby, came to see me and charge the atmosphere with her prayers. I'm sure it was difficult for her to see me like that, but as the God-fearing woman that she is, she did not allow her emotions prevent her from her assignment to pray for me. It was also Neah who on another occasion called to pray over the phone. I'm told that I had reacted when she was praying and as the days passed and I was still in a coma, one of the doctors asked if someone could ask Neah to call and pray again.

During the time that I was in the hospital, Neah's grandmother passed away and her grandfather had passed away the prior year. As we shared a meal months after I was released from the hospital, she said to me that she prayed for God to spare my life and heal my body and she knew it could be done. But…she added that after the recent losses of her grandparents "I don't know what it would have done to us if you had passed too. We needed you to make it." Neah was able to see the prayers of her and her family answered.

Praying in the midst of Loss is powerful!

WHERE IS OUR PATIENT ON THIS CHART?

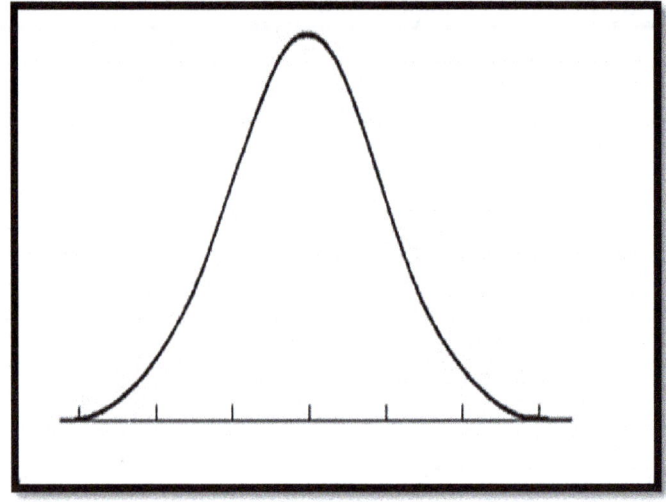

Thanksgiving is a trigger for my family and some others in that it reminds them about the Thanksgiving they spent in the Hospital with me or if not physically at the hospital, thinking about or praying for me. It was the night before Thanksgiving 2019, and me and my cousins Donne' and Dari had meal prep items all over the kitchen; there was hardly an empty surface. At one point, Dari and I were in the kitchen alone and we laughed and talked with music playing in the background just in case we had to take a break and dance like we would sometimes do. W reflected on the previous year when I walked into the emergency room with her and her husband Robert not to leave until 6 weeks later.

Here we were doing what she, her sister Donne' and I had done for so many years in the kitchen of their parents' home. Based on my medical prognosis a year earlier, I certainly should not have been able to cook, talk, and laugh as though nothing had occurred. But God!!!

I have noticed that when some people who were involved in my situation talk to me about that period, they talk as though they are still processing things. During these times I would hear information or perspectives that I had never heard. This night was one of those times. As Dari chopped vegetables, she reflected aloud and proclaimed, "This is when it became real to me!" I listened quietly waiting for her to explain what she meant. She was referring to the moment when she realized what actually happened to me on the night I was admitted to the ICU. Like many of the hospitals in DC, the hospital where I was admitted is a teaching hospital. Dari told me that one of the days when she was visiting me, she heard a revelatory conversation between the lead doctor and the Residents who were gathered around my bed discussing my case. At this time, I was still on life-support, and she recalls that I was still in the medically induced coma. Standing in front of a white board, the lead doctor drew a bell curve with a line starting from the bottom left corner and going up to the highest point on the board at the center and coming back down to the lowest point on the right side. After drawing the illustration, the doctor referring to me asked the Residents "where was our patient on this chart?" Their eyes scanned the chart and as they quietly thought about the question, the lead doctor maybe a little impatient with the delay in responses answered his own question. He said, "Our patient was off the chart!" "She died!"

My cousin told me this as she shook her head saying, "That's when it became real!" Those words hit her like a ton of bricks at the time and had the same effect on me a year later as she told me the story. While most of the medical personnel talked about my past and current condition using complicated medical terminology, this doctor…on this day…made it plain and simple. He said, I had died. I was speechless as I listened to Dari. In my private time that evening, I pictured the scenario and pondered the thoughts. "Wow. I was off the chart but now I'm alive! Thanks be to God!!"

> *"The gift of life should not be taken for granted."*

BOOK OF ESTHER: PERHAPS I WAS THERE FOR A PURPOSE

As I lay in my ICU bed one night with Janice by me, I heard and recognized their voices as they entered the space. It was Genell and Neah; mother and daughter friends; family not by blood. I remember that my eyes were closed though I am pretty sure I could have opened them. During this period of my time in ICU, I was conscious. Well, at least I was in and out of consciousness and I didn't have tubes down my throat. I was not yet allowed to take in food because I had not passed the 'swallow test.' It was so good to hear the sound of their voices. I thought that I heard the voice of Amara as well; Genell's other daughter, but she was not in the room. Perhaps I heard her on the phone. At the time, I actually thought that Neah and Genell were also on the phone. It was not until months after I was discharged and was discussing the visit with Genell that she told me that she and Neah were in the room with me that night. I had greatly improved by the time of their visit. Janice can attest to that fact, but Genell told me that from her perspective, I looked as though I "was on my way home." In other words, she did not think I was long for this world, but she still wanted to read to me from the Bible. Her desire to read to me was strong, I would later find out, and it was not a general desire and it was not a general desire where she would just select a popular and encouraging passage. No, she specifically wanted to read from the Book of Esther. The Book of Esther was not an easy read, especially in the heavily sedated state I was in. Although it is not a long book with only 10 Chapters, it contains a dense historical account with many twists and complexities. I will not discuss or share analyses that have been done on this book of the Bible found in the Old Testament but on a very high level, it concerns a Jewish maiden who during a time when the people of Israel were in exile in Persia, was able to become the queen of Persia with the assistance of an uncle named Mordecai and after going through a long preparatory process with other maidens who were hopeful of being the one that would be chosen Queen. Once she became Queen, Esther kept her Jewish heritage a secret from the King. In her unique position as queen of Persia, she was able to be used to deliver her people, the Jews, from being massacred.

Genell asked Neah to read certain verses and then Genell expounded on them. I remember hearing them read. Although I was familiar with the story, in my sedated state it was a lot of words for me to process. At one point as she was expounding, Genell tried to recall the name of Esther's uncle and it didn't come to her mind. She said, "I can't remember his name right now...what was his name?" She then addressed me and said, "Charlma you probably know his name." Despite not being fully engaged with what was going on, I heard Genell's question to me and I responded aloud "Mordecai". She responded, "yes, that's his name; Mordecai." I continued listening but did not say anything else. I also remember how insistent Genell was to continue reading. She did not seem to care that I was not responding. I recall at the time wondering why she was so intent on reading that account and I asked her that question a couple of times, months and even more than a year after leaving the hospital. Her response both times was that she did not know why she chose to read the Book of Esther, or why she was so focused on reading it to me even though I did not look well, but that she felt it was important for her to read it. I pondered that question myself many times. Just like Genell felt it was important for her to read from that portion of scripture, I thought it was very significant that it is the only scripture read to me when I was in ICU that I recall being read I am told that reading from the Bible was something that regularly went on while I was in ICU. I have even been told that I would react in some way like opening my eyes, trying to lift up, or moving my foot when I heard the Word of God read and songs of praise sung or played. While I remember one of the songs in particular that was often played when I was in ICU, I do not recall any of the scriptures, except for the Book of Esther.

One of the most quoted portions from the Book of Esther comes from the account when her uncle Mordecai referring to her being both a Jewish woman whose people were in captivity and the Queen of the nation that held her people captive, said the following:

> *"For if you keep silent at this time, relief and deliverance will rise for the Jews from another place, but you and your father's house will perish. And who knows whether you have not come to the kingdom for such a time as this?"*
> Esther 4:14

As I continued listening to Neah and Genell read, I remember at one-point Genell said "this is the part I want you to hear" and either she or Neah read the above quoted language. Hmmm. On the surface there is absolutely nothing that I had in common with Queen Esther. My being in an ICU critically ill could not be further from the stature of royalty that she had been elevated to. Her becoming Queen was a coveted personal advancement for her and she had been selected among many. In contrast, there was nothing about the condition I was in that was chosen nor was it seen as an advancement in my life. I was flat on my back and from the perspective of the doctors, I continued to straddle between life and death.

While Esther's fellow Jewish people likely looked to her as their inroad to gain the mercy of the King, no one was looking to my situation to provide any benefit to them. The most they had been asking was that I open my eyes...that I respond in a way that the doctors would acknowledge. Yet, I know that it was not just a coincidence that Genell was so determined to have that quoted language from the Book of Esther read to me. It was also not a coincidence that I remembered that the passages were read and even participated by being able to respond to Genell's question about it, all while I had my eyes closed and was heavily sedated. God is not random and there are no coincidences with Him. So, what was it about this seemingly unrelated account? What was the 'why'?

I believe the similarity between me, and Queen Esther was simply that we both occupied positions that could benefit others. It was obvious how Esther's position could benefit others, but mine; not so much. Even though there is no similarity in where we were; she was in a palace, and I was in a hospital. It was our positions, nonetheless. The power of our positions. Stay with me. What I mean is that, because Esther was in the palace and because she had favor with the king, her people...the people of Israel could and did benefit in a way that they would not have but for Esther being in the palace married to the king and able to request favors. Esther interceded on their behalf before the king. I can hear some of you saying "Yes, I get it as far as Esther goes. She was royalty and in a powerful position and she used that position to profoundly benefit a nation. But...Charlma... back to you! What is the similarity?

Unlike Esther, I certainly did not take any courageous action; I in fact did nothing. But through seeing me on life support with little expectation of survival, praying for me then seeing me dramatically revived and restored, many people had the opportunity to be profoundly changed and to have hope in future situations when they may not otherwise have had hope. These are things I've been told by some of the witnesses. Do not misunderstand what I am saying. As I mentioned early on in this book, God did not make me ill but in the midst of my situation, God made ways when there seemed to be no way...when the doctors told my loved ones that there was nothing else they could do and that I wasn't improving enough and that life support should be removed, and that my brain functioning would be diminished, and that I could not live independently...and...and God worked miracles!

After hearing and continuing to hear so many testimonies from some of the direct witnesses who saw me firsthand at my worse and then in the months afterwards, it is clear that my position as grim as it looked, was a position of power just like Esther's was, and it was used as a platform for God's miracle to elevate the faith of some and at a minimum, the mindsets of others. What God has done for me has served as a means for non-believers to believe, the faith of Believers to grow higher, for medical professionals to see that despite the limitations of what science says that there is more; always more beyond them that can determine the destiny of a patient in their care, and for others to believe in miracles in the midst of darkness.

Perhaps, just perhaps, during my time in ICU ....my position and the participation of others was used by God "for such a time as this."

> *"Any position or circumstance can be used by God to elevate and empower you and others."*

SECTION VI
The Miracle: Ripple Effect

"A miracle is not a 'one and done' occurrence; it is a supernatural event that has long term impact."

THE RIPPLE EFFECT: MORE THAN THEY EXPECTED/ BARGAINED FOR

I don't know about you, but I get a thrill out of going to a place for a specific purpose and ending up receiving a benefit that I wasn't expecting. Like setting out to make a quick trip to the grocery store and while there, seeing an old friend that you haven't seen in many years and the two of you spend time in the middle of the store catching up. It is a surprise; an unexpected benefit; a blessing! Receiving the unexpected happened to many people who came to the ICU to see me. They were told that if they wanted to see me, they should come. My condition was critical, and time was of the essence. After I made it through the first night, some were asked to come and pray, play music, or talk to me. Just like it is on those occasions when we set out to do one thing and something unexpected happens that shifts us, changes us, or impacts our lives in some way, so it was for some who visited me in the ICU. They got more than they bargained for...they received the unexpected.

Many people have shared their experiences with me about what they saw, heard, and participated in while visiting me in the ICU. It seems to me that what some people experienced depended on who was there and what was going on during their visit. Some have told me that they were personally encouraged and edified seeing the power of God in action as prayers and praise and worship filled the space. Some of the visitors received prayer as my friends and church family who were praying for me turned their attention to the needs of others in the room. One person told me that once when I was being anointed with oil and prayed for that, others in the room including one of the nurses asked to be prayed for as well. Another friend told me "You know, we were coming in shifts, and I wanted to visit during the shift where the people were praying and singing." Why was it that she wanted to be there at that time? It was because she knew that she would reap the benefits of the prayer and praise being in an atmosphere where the presence of God was, even if it was an ICU. A different friend describing the atmosphere of the ICU when she had visited me said "it was like church in there. People were praying and singing." For sure, she was not expecting that when she came to visit, but as she told me about it, it was obvious that she had been blessed by what she experienced. Another person told me that they could feel the presence of God in the place.

Many months after I had been released from the hospital, a friend who would soon be going to the hospital for the birth of her baby was putting together her song list to listen to while she was in labor. She told me there was a song that was being played for me during one of her visits to the ICU and she said "I have to have that song on my playlist! She had been greatly moved by the particular worship song and knew it would be an encouragement to her while she was in labor. Did she expect to be encouraged and listening to praise and worship music when she came to the ICU to see me? Probably not, but in the midst of the situation that brought her to the hospital, she was. I mentioned the name of a song that I remembered hearing when I was said to have been non-responsive and she said "Yes, that's it!" A year after I left the hospital and was sharing a meal with my friend Sonya, she told me that she missed how everyday my friend Linda would send out messages and that people would come together and pray. They focused on different areas like 'today, let's pray for Charlma's liver' Or, let's pray that she can pass the swallow test. Sonya said that it was nice. Sometime later I asked her what it was that impacted her about those community prayers, and she said it was "the togetherness every day."

Some of the people who came to visit and pray for me have told me about the impact of that period on their faith walk. Some have shared that their faith has increased, and their 'increased faith' has remained even though in some other situations their prayers have not always been answered in the manner that they would want. My friend Temaki told me that the Lord released a higher level of anointing on her life that was necessary to address the situations she encountered in the ICU with me and everyone else. My situation was hard, and my condition was critical, so her faith had to be at a higher level. My pastor also told me that his faith was different because of that experience. Even though I did not look like myself when he saw me in ICU, he told me he never believed that I was not going to make it. He said that when he was in the ICU, he had to move away from the people in the room who were reciting the 'facts and statistics. He said that the experience of my miracle has caused him to pray differently for people, increased his faith and made him more of a fighter. He talked to me about his increased faith even though in the two years after I left the hospital, he and his family lost four loved ones who we also prayed for but who did not survive. Also, a dear brother in the Lord who visited me while I was in the hospital who we all prayed for, including my pastor, as he battled cancer passed away shortly after I was released.

Nonetheless, in the face of these situations that did not turn out like mine, my pastor has not stopped acknowledging that God is still a healer and will publicly say referring to me and a dear friend of his who also was raised up after being critically ill in the ICU that "we have seen God heal! Another friend, in discussing his current relationship with God recently told me that he was on his own faith journey and had been focused on it the last couple of years. Referring to what he witnessed with the miracle God performed in my life, he said "I know that God is real and know what He can do!" My situation served as a catalyst for him to examine his own life from a different perspective.

These are examples of some who got more than they bargained for in the process of coming to my side and interceding on my behalf. My prayer is that they always hold on to what they experienced.

> "Don't try to anticipate how God is going to bless you in a situation. There is always more than meets the eye."

THE RIPPLE EFFECT: NEW BOLDNESS CAME FORTH

I believe that when James 5:16 says that the effectual fervent prayer of the righteous availeth much…," the 'much' that is gained is not just in relation to the situation or person being prayed for, but the much gained is also for the person/people doing the praying. I am convinced that all those who prayed for me gained something whether they prayed in person, on the phone or from other continents.

I've shared elsewhere in this book that the members of my church participated in a 24-hour prayer rotation. Each of them was assigned a one-hour block of time to pray for me. A sacrifice that I'm so grateful for. I've heard testimonies from some of those who prayed telling of what happened to them when they were praying for me. One person told me their prayer life had risen to a higher level because they had never prayed that long for a situation that did not directly involve them. Someone else said that as they prayed for me, the Holy Spirit brought other needs before them that they then prayed for and before they knew it, an hour had passed. For another woman, a bold prophetic voice was released in her that she had not previously experienced. This section is about her.

About two weeks before I was released from the hospital, I came upon a text message from a young woman from my church to me where she shared what she heard the Lord saying to her during one of her one-hour prayer slots. When she sent it, I was still in a coma, so I didn't see it until a month after it was written. In the face of the reports that I might not survive, this is what she wrote:

> *"GOD GAVE ME THE SCRIPTURE BELOW AND THE HOLY SPIRIT IS MOVING RIGHT NOW TO AFFIRM OUR CONFIDENCE – MAY IT BE IN YOU, AND IN ALL THOSE AROUND YOU AND IN ALL OF THOSE PRAYING FOR YOU. THE HOLY SPIRIT IS MOVING THROUGH EVERY PERSON THAT KNOWS YOU AND ENCOUNTERING YOU. GODS PLAN IS AT WORK! I LOVE YOU MY DEAR SIS CHARLMA AND BY HIS GRACE, HIS WORD, AND THROUGH THE POWER OF WORSHIP AND PRAYER MAY YOU HAVE PEACE AND CONFIDENCE IN ALL THAT OUR GOD CAN AND WILL DO."*

The Scripture she had been given was I John 5:13-15 NKJV:

> *13 These things I have written to you who believe in the name of the Son of God, that you may know that you have eternal life, and that*

you may continue to believe in the name of the Son of God. 14 Now this is the confidence that we have in Him, that if we ask anything according to His will, He hears us. 15 And if we know that He hears us, whatever we ask, we know that we have the petitions that we have asked of Him.

When I saw the text, I was taken aback by how boldly she declared that God's plan was at work. Through her words, she expressed a knowing that God was not only working on my behalf but was also moving on behalf of everyone around me who was praying. Two weeks after seeing the text, I went to church and saw the woman who had sent it. I told her how bold, powerful, and prophetic her declaration of faith was. As I said "Wow," she shook her head with her eyes closed with a slight tear falling and said "I've never done that before. It's not me. God brought something out of me during the time I was praying for you. It was all God." This was a profound example of how God was moving in the people praying for me in ways that had nothing to do with me. My situation just presented the opportunity for God to release things…to stir up and bring forth spiritual gifts.

This indeed was the testimony of this young woman who had obediently prayed for me. Her effectual and fervent prayers availed much for her!

> *"Praying for someone else during their trials can release unexpected gifts in you."*

THE RIPPLE EFFECT: CONFIDENCE WAS RELEASED IN ME THAT NIGHT

At this point, it was three years since Michelle had been sent to the ICU with her cousin Justin to pray for me. Three years since she witnessed God bring me from a position of near death to a position of abundant life. As we were on the phone having one of our marathon conversations that resulted from us not talking for a long time, we had to cover all topics and at some point the conversation went to my time in ICU. I asked her whether seeing me in that state caused her to think that I would not survive. She responded that, while she wanted to believe that I would survive, looking at me... hearing what was being said and seeing the various machines that I was hooked up to, she didn't see how I could survive. Michelle was clear, however, that being in the hospital praying for me was where she and her cousin needed to be and what they needed to do. She also knew that they needed to keep coming back. Michelle said that as she kept coming back, she was amazed at how quickly God was restoring me even when those attending to me did not see the restoration that she saw.

The reason I am including an account about Michelle in this chapter on the ripple effect is because during the conversation we were having, it was the first time she ever shared with me some specific impacts she experienced years later that resulted from her going to pray for me despite her initial feelings of reluctance and feeling unqualified. In talking about going to the hospital to pray for me, she said:

> *"That was the first time that I knew and felt so strongly that God could use me in that way; to pray out loud for someone like that in public. That experience gave me something deeper about myself that I did not know was there. It opened something up!"*

She explained further that her initial act of obedience to go to the hospital and pray opened up something and prepared her for some other experiences in the future. She shared that when my Godson Amir came to visit and was in the hallway because he did not want to see me in the state I was in, that she talked to him, and he agreed to go into the room. His mother Linda then asked Michelle if she would pray with them by my bed. So, Michelle was again being asked to pray aloud. She said that after the prayer, Linda shared with her that she felt it was helpful and that she felt better. Michelle said she remembered thinking "Wow God, you really are using me!"

This new area that Michelle was stepping into did not stop in my ICU room. She told me that the next year one of her senior family members who held a position of leadership in his church was sick, she visited him. Michelle said that during one visit she asked him whether it would be ok if she prayed for him. She shared that throughout her life she had been prayed for by him, and prior to what God released in her in my ICU room, she never would have asked to pray for him, because it was not her 'place' she would have thought. Based on what Michelle shared with me, I imagine her family member was surprised that she even asked, but he responded "yes" to her request, and she began to pray with power! It appears the flood gates had been opened because she said during another visit to see her family, there was a man in the waiting room who had come to visit his son who had been in a horrible accident and that the doctors did not expect him to be able to walk because so much was shattered in his body. Just as she had with her family member, Michelle asked this man if it would be ok if she prayed for him and his son. He agreed, and she prayed boldly for his son's healing. Some days later during another one of her visits there, she was sitting in the waiting area when the man she had prayed for walked in. He excitedly told her that he was hoping that he would see her so that he could tell her how well his son was doing. He reported that his son was able to get out of the bed and move around and the man believed that her prayers contributed to his recovery! Michelle said to me:

> *"If I had not gone to the ICU that night to pray for you, I would never have had the confidence to pray like that for a stranger's healing and participate in what God was doing!"*

Indeed, what was released when she was in my ICU room was for a lifetime, not just for that moment.

> *"When God releases power in you for a situation, it is for more than just that moment."*

THE RIPPLE EFFECT: WHAT IS GOING ON HERE?

It was about 7:30 pm and my room on the step-down unit was quiet as it typically was in the evening when I did not have visitors. She walked into my room and when she saw me, she smiled her beautiful trademark smile. We chatted for about five minutes by my estimation and then as though something all of the sudden dawned on her, she asked as she sweepingly moving her hands, "What is going on here?" I was not sure what she meant by the question when she asked it. She wasn't quite sure what was happening, or rather, not happening in my room. I could tell that she was not really expecting an answer from me as it was a rhetorical question. She had been in my room for a while, looked around, and noticed how quiet it was.

Although I love music, I wasn't playing any. It was still...and quiet. This visitor was incredibly happy to see me coherent, sitting up in the bed and talking as she had been in the ICU when it was questionable whether I was going to make it out alive, let alone, be able to engage with her as I was. But it was the explanation that followed the statement "what is going on here?!" that let me know she was looking to experience something that she had experienced before.

She told me "When you were in ICU people were coming and going praying and singing, it was like church in there." There it was; she had benefited from the ripple effect of what was going on in the ICU and received something unexpected that fed her spirit and soul. So now, as she stood in my room looking around, it was quiet...it was different. I believe that visiting me to check on my progress was the priority, but I believe she was also hoping for a repeat of what she had experienced when she visited me in the ICU. She wanted to experience again the power of prayer and the praise because it clearly had done something for her. Strengthened her perhaps... touched her as only the presence of God can do. Hence, her question "What is going on here" was a recognition that something had changed...that this was not the same atmosphere she experienced before.

There was a difference in my room that night; but then there wasn't. What I mean is that God was still at work, but how the presence of God was operating had shifted. The fact that I was upright, in my right mind and able to speak, to think and to engage with her was evidence that a shift had occurred. A shift from near death to life. Whether it clicked for her then or not, sitting before her was a manifestation of God's grace and mercy and the power of prayer. The things that had been prayed for in the ICU had come to past! Yes, there had been a shift...the atmosphere had changed, but nothing was lacking!

> "God is constantly doing new things, don't get comfortable with what he was doing yesterday."

Photo Credits: Susan King Beneventi

SECTION VII
Me; Throughout the Process

YOU DON'T BELONG HERE

"For I know the thoughts that I think toward you, saith the LORD, thoughts of peace, and not of evil, to give you an expected end." Jeremiah 29:11

"You don't belong here" she said to me softly as she shook her head from left to right. Very soon after being transferred out of ICU into a private room, one of the precious nurses assigned to me introduced herself and started getting things in order in my room, checking my vital signs, and getting me water. She then stopped and looked at me with a serious expression and asked me if she could pray for me. I was so grateful that she asked, and I responded yes without any hesitation. She quietly prayed over me and although I could not hear all of the words, I did hear her ask for God to heal me. After the nurse finished praying, she looked at me and said, "You don't belong here." She didn't provide any explanation for the statement and after saying what "you don't belong here", she completed her tasks in my room and left. Although she came to my room many times after that during the weeks that I was in the hospital, she never uttered those words again and she did not pray out loud for me again.

In speaking those words to me, the nurse did not mean that I was not sick enough to be in the hospital because she along with everyone else was monitoring my condition and providing medical treatment. In those initial days, I did not even have enough strength to push a button on the nurse call system, open a bottle, not to mention that I couldn't feed myself, walk, lift my arms or legs, turn over on my side, or much else. Her comment was not based on what she was seeing in front of her because as a Christian she knew that the Bible says we are to "walk by faith, not by sight."[23] Her comment was made with the knowledge that God's plan for me was that I be well; that I be raised from this bed of affliction, just as God had raised me out of the coma in the ICU and brought me to the point where my organs were functioning again. Her comment showed that she understood that Jesus had more for me to do in this life and that he had not brought me through all that I had experienced up to that point so I could stay in a hospital bed in the condition I was in. What she really meant was that the state I was in was not how I was to stay.

I didn't express it to this nurse, but I agreed that I did not belong in that hospital bed. I was so thankful to God for sending me that encouragement! Regardless of all my limitations at that time and what she saw from a medical standpoint, that nurse could see with eyes of faith that I

---

[23] II Corinthians 5:7.

didn't belong there; that God's plan was that I be healed and out of the hospital. She was correct...sort of. What I mean is, the fact that God's plan was that I be healed does not mean that the path I was on, being in the hospital struggling to push a button, unable to walk or feed myself, was not supposed to happen. For many people, witnessing the broken state I was in and then the miraculous state I was later in is what strengthened their faith or caused them to believe in the power of God when they previously did not. The issue is that the process or the journey to the place God intends, rarely looks like we think it should look. Some Christians expect to be able to just slide into the promises of God without any obstacles and hardships. While that certainly can, and does happen, it often does not, yet the struggle or obstacle is still a move of God. Clearly, God did not put me in that hospital bed, but my journey was allowed, and the situation was used for good. So, from that aspect, being in that bed was exactly where I belonged at that time. It just did not represent the condition I would end up in. The benefits gained from me being there would be revealed in the days, weeks, and years to come. They continued being revealed to me even as I wrote this book.

When I hear comments from people who witnessed my ordeal and experienced me afterward say things like "I know that God is real"; "I saw what God can do"; "I sort of believed in God before, but I do believe in God now"; or "You are a miracle", I know that indeed, I really did belong right where I was at that time so I could be a living testimony that Jesus is still a miracle worker.

> *"Whenever God works a miracle in a person's life, it is never just about them."*

I WAS NOT FIGHTING FOR MY LIFE; GOD WAS IN CONTROL

<u>Will to Live:</u> *"desire, determination, and effort to survive." Nursing Outcomes Classification: "The sense of self-preservation, usually coupled to a future sense- i.e. dreams, aspirations, and expectations for future improvement in one's state in life." Segen's Medical Dictionary, 2012.*

My testimony is not one of those remarkable 'will to live' stories where a person who is critically ill or in another precarious situation fights hard with unwavering determination to overcome and survive the situation. Indeed, the human constitution is phenomenal and most of us have heard or read accounts of people overcoming unimaginable hardships and challenges because of their drive to survive, that is, their will to live. I am inspired by those accounts and so admire those people, but I am compelled to tell you that is not my story. No matter how it may have looked to some, when I was at my worst in the ICU, it was not my strength, my courage, or my will to live that raised me up. It was the power of God who answered prayers and totally changed my expected outcome because death was never God's plan for me at that time!

There are those who, despite either seeing or hearing about my condition and the prognosis that I would likely be severely physically and/or mentally impacted if I survived, cannot wrap their head around an explanation that points to divine intervention from God as the reason I was fully functional within a short period of leaving the hospital. In my context, fully functional included living independently, navigating public transportation, walking miles per day, fully engaging with people, resuming a professional career that requires me to assess, analyze and reach conclusions about complicated matters and effectively balance multiple projects at the same time.[24] In their view, it was my strength, my fortitude and my will to live that had a large part in my recovery or the miracle that I talked about. So, I've heard statements like "You were fighting for your life."; "You're such a fighter"; "You are so strong", "I knew if anyone would make it, it would be you." While these statements make sense and apply to some people in some situations, I cannot take credit for having these attributes. I was not responsible for my kidneys resuming their function or me coming back from a lifeless state. Also, the 'will to live' as defined at the beginning of this segment includes "the desire, determination, and effort to survive" and the "sense of self-

---

[24] Two days after I was released from the hospital, I was able to take a subway train in Washington, DC navigating within the two-level subway station.

preservation, usually coupled to a future sense- i.e., dreams, aspirations, and expectations for future improvement in one's state in life." Most of these attributes require a conscious mind or that decision making that is intact. None of this was my state of mind. There was a progression of the degree of consciousness that I experienced in ICU. I went from not conscious at all to being somewhat conscious of things around me but still in a non-verbal state. Even at that somewhat conscious/non-verbal point, I felt no pain or stress and did not have any awareness that I was in a critical situation that required that I fight to come out of it. Still later, when I progressed to a state where I heard some conversations and was keenly aware that I was thirsty and not being given any water, I did not have the strength to strive.

Now, don't misunderstand me here. I am not saying that I don't possess the will to live or fight because once I was transferred from ICU to a regular room, I tried my best to get stronger by eating food such as chicken and fish which I would have never eaten prior to being hospitalized. I pushed myself to do simple things like stand up and walk again. And, after leaving the hospital, I practiced walking up stairs every day because that was my greatest struggle. In fact, by the end of January 2019, the month I was released from the hospital, I had climbed over 100 steps.[25] However, what I am saying is that in my most critical state, it was God, not any will to live or effort on my part that raised me up.

Despite what I've described above, I end this segment by saying that for those people who were blessed or greatly encouraged by what they "perceived" was my decision to 'fight', I am so thankful they were encouraged. I heard from a very dear friend that seeing me fight helped them want to push forward and live when they were going through a really difficult time. To that I say Thank You Jesus! Thank you for using my situation to encourage another.

> *"God was fighting my battle, not me."*

---

[25] In an instant message to a friend who asked how I was doing, I responded "Working on increasing my strength. I climbed over 100 stairs yesterday. Day by day...God is restoring me..."

DREAMS

I recently mentioned to a friend that I am a dreamer. Their response was "What do you mean? Doesn't everyone dream?" Her comment was correct because according to science, regardless of what people think about whether they dream, everyone dreams.[26] The issue is that not everyone remembers their dreams. A more accurate statement would have been that I remember a lot of my dreams and have throughout my life, even some from when I was a very young child. So, the fact that I was dreaming while I was in the hospital does not surprise me. There were times when I was in ICU that I knew that I was dreaming, but there were other times that I did not know that I had dreamed about a certain event until I later asked those involved whether the event had actually happened. I have mentioned some of these situations in other chapters such as when I thought my Godson Amir leaned close to my ear and as though he were giving me a pep talk said, "This isn't too hard for you to get through is it?" In other words, he was declaring that my situation was not too hard for me to get through. Or, when I thought two of my

---

[26] See, for example Dreams, Sleep Foundation, Eric Suni (medically reviewed by Alex Dimitriu, Psychiatrist), December 15, 2022; "Does Everyone Dream?", Discover-By Neuroskeptic, Sep. 1, 2015.

colleagues who had visited were walking around my bed with a Bible open and reciting the Lord's Prayer. I had many other dreams and I have fond memories about them all.

I've heard of critically ill patients having wild dreams or hallucinations while in the hospital. Some of the experiences are very frightening. There is even something called ICU delirium where patients experience symptoms like paranoia, fear, nightmares, and hallucination. Research suggests that as many as 80% of ICU patients experience ICU delirium.[27] I have no idea how the dreams I had at times during my time in ICU would be classified but they were never frightening. There was nothing negative at all. To the contrary, the dreams were always embedded with biblical scripture, an encouraging word, a direction, a beautiful scene, or something else supportive to me. I am thankful that even in my dreams, God shielded me from terror!

---

[27] Hallucinations Confusion Dizziness Symptoms of ICU Delirium, article by Matthew Schreiber, MD, Associate Director, Medical ICU and Attending Physician, Pulmonary Disease/Critical Care, December 04, 2018; Hospitals struggle to address terrifying and long-lasting 'ICU delirium', article by Usha Lee McFarling, STAT, October 14, 2016.

> The bible tells us that we do not need to be afraid of the terrors of night (Psalm 91:5).
> I believe this... I am a witness!

SUA SPONTE

One of many terms of Latin origin used in the legal profession is *sua sponte* defined as "on its own will or on its own motion…" A more straight forward definition is "at its own prompting; by its own impulse; of its own free will." You may ask "Why is she talking about some archaic Latin term that lawyers use? What is the point?" When I heard accounts about what was happening to my body at times and read comments from my medical record, the term *sua sponte* came to my mind in the context of my miraculous recovery. For example, when my kidneys weren't functioning and the dialysis was not working well, the doctors did not know what to do at one point. I talk about this more in another chapter[28], but people specifically prayed for my kidneys to function, and they did. While to some it may have seemed that they just started working *sua sponte*, I submit to you that the prayers were the catalyst bringing forth the change. Another situation that occurred in my body was that there was inflammation of my large intestine as a result of inadequate blood supply. The medical notes do not say that the bleeding ceased because XYZ treatment was administered. Instead, they state that the bleeding stopped "by itself, without any

---

[28] "Let it Flow Like the River Jordan", Section IV.

intervention." This is because the doctors had no other explanation. They knew that it was not a result of anything they did, so they concluded the bleeding must have stopped on its own somehow. Again, while it may have appeared that the issue with my intestine was resolved *sua sponte* on its own impulse, I say absolutely not! The prayers went forth and God intervened!

> "There were things going on that could not be intellectually explained."

MY REHABILITATION

"Many are the plans in a person's heart, but it is the LORD'S purpose that prevails." Proverbs 19:21.

"What do you mean I can't go to the rehab facility you told me about?!" I was frustrated because none of my top choices, or any choices for that matter, for rehabilitation were working out. The social worker who I asked the question to told me that since I could now walk a certain number of yards without assistance, I could not go to the highly skilled location that several people had recommended to me. This was despite the fact that one of the doctors who was assessing my post-hospital needs had told me she suggested a rigorous placement for me after having observed me during my second therapy session in the hospital gym and seeing how difficult it was for me to go up four steps and the unsteadiness of my walking even with assistance. But it had been a week and a half since the time she had observed me, and I had improved. The social worker had been reading the physical therapy notes from my in-house sessions. I also remembered him remarking one day as I slowly walked down the hospital corridor holding on to a walker with a nurse following behind me, "You're doing well." I was thrilled I had improved from the 3 steps that I was able to take a couple of weeks before, but I couldn't believe that because I could take cautious steps down a hall holding onto a walker and wearing a leather belt around my waist so the physical therapist could hold onto to me, I was considered to be 'walking unassisted'. Let me go back to provide a little context for the comment made about the rehab. A couple of weeks after I moved from ICU to the 'step down' patient room, one focus was identifying an appropriate rehab for me. The social work staff at the hospital provided a list of places and family and friends provided recommendations. There was one location that several people recommended that had a great reputation for helping patients advance. This rehab was consistently rated number one; I wanted to go there! I wasn't able to get a spot in this facility, so the second place on my list was pursued. It was this selection that I was told would not be a fit for me. Now what? I thought. It was like my progress was causing me to advance beyond the various rehabilitation locations. I was happy about my progress, but the plan I had for my post-hospital rehabilitation was breaking down. At least that is what I thought. In actuality, what was happening is that God's plan was going to replace the plan I thought I needed.

At some point during the second week that I was in my patient room, the nurses started putting me in a chair next to my bed some days for as long as I could stand it before getting tired. At this point I couldn't walk or stand up on my own for that matter. While my family and I continued to check into rehab facilities, I began physical therapy in the hospital. They started with helping me stand up. I remember the first time the therapist put me in a chair and said "Now, stand up." I wasn't able to. My mind knew what to do but I did not have the strength to stand. As days went by, she started telling me to count to four slowly and when I reached four, she would help pull me up. This continued until one day I was able to count to four and then stand up on my own. What a victory that was! This was also around the time that I could sit in a chair (rather than in the bed) for most of the day.

At the beginning of January, I was told that the staff was working to release me in the next few days. I had been in the hospital for six weeks and was so happy to leave. That week, the doctor on my medical team that was to approve my rehabilitation plan and sign my release papers came to check on me. Earlier in my stay, she had tried to make the case for me to go to a facility as I had wanted and as she agreed would be good for me, but now as she reviewed the most recent notes from my therapy session in the hospital, she said that she could not justify a facility for me. She told me that based on my progress, having therapy at home would be best for me. It is so interesting when I look back at that period; the last two weeks before I was released. I was so consumed with going to a facility and hearing my loved ones tell me how I really needed to go somewhere[29] that I was totally missing what God was doing...how I was being restored so quickly...how God continued to work miraculously in me. I recall how I went from not being able to push a button, open a bottle, turn my body from one side to the other, stand up, walk, or take care of any of my personal needs to being able to bath and feed myself, and walk down the hall of the hospital with a walker. A week and a half before I was discharged, one nurse in particular pushed me with gentleness telling me that I should try to walk to the bathroom that was three feet from my bed. From that day on, that is what I did. I remember people visiting me one week and then the following week commenting on how much better I was able to feed myself since their last visit. I was making progress. God was still at work.

---

[29] Regarding the need for intense therapy, at some point I made a comment about not needing the level of therapy that everyone thought. My friend Kathy told me "You have to see it from our perspective. We saw you." In other words, some of them had seen me at my worst and knew that I would have to receive a lot of assistance to be properly rehabilitated.

The day before I was to leave, the doctor who would release me came to go over procedures such as the doctors I was to schedule appointments with when I left and the medication I should take until the doctors said otherwise. As anxious as I was to leave, I was a little apprehensive because her instructions to me were very routine. They did not sound like instructions that would be given to someone who statistically shouldn't even be alive. I figured there must be something more. I asked her "Do you have any special instructions? Do I have any limitations? She stopped and looked at me and said, "What do you mean by limitations?" I responded, "You know, do I have limitations like not picking up anything too heavy? Or not going places?" She bluntly said, "No. You don't have limitations. You had this happen to you, you are stable. You're uncomfortable because you've been here so long. You just need to get out of the hospital and live your life."

The day had finally come when I would leave the hospital! I could not wait to feel the fresh air on my face. Sheila, one of "the Girls"[30], willingly volunteered to pick me up and take me to my friend Linda's apartment; Linda opened up her place to me and I was to take physical

---

[30] See the segment on "The Girls."

therapy from there. On that day I was wheeled out of the hospital to Sheila's car. I had a brand-new walker that I was to use in the months to come. When we arrived at the apartment, I got out of the car and started walking slowly up the walkway and into the building. Something felt strange to me. After being enclosed in a room for a period of time, I recall the feeling of having no barriers around me as I slowly walked. I held on to the railing as I navigated the six steps that led to the hallway leading to the apartment. I was in Linda's apartment for a few hours before I realized that I did not have the walker! I had mistakenly left it at the hospital which means that from the time I had gotten out of the car until I got to the apartment door, I had walked on my own without the crutch I had used in the hospital. I guess the absence of any equipment was what felt strange to me. To this day, the walker still has the tags on it as I have never had to use it.

On Sunday, two days after I was released from the hospital, I decided to go to my church in Maryland and surprise everyone. I know it sounds a little crazy since I had just gotten out of the hospital, but I was free and ready to go. I thought about my route carefully in my head: I would take an Uber to the Metro, walk down the escalator to the platform where the train would come, then I would get off at the metro station in Maryland and go down the escalator, and walk slowly to the car of my friend Lorna who attended my church and who I would ask to pick me up. I figured that even if I got tired as I walked in the metro station, there were enough things to lean on. The plan worked perfectly except that when I had pictured my route in my head, I forgot that the Metro station in Washington, DC that I went to required additional walking because it had two levels of escalators that I had to go down instead of just one like I pictured it. I was able to do it easily and I thanked God for giving me the strength! When I arrived at the Metro station in Maryland where Lorna was to meet me, I walked out towards the parking lot towards her car. When she saw me, she rushed from her car towards me and said, "I saw you walking, so I didn't think that was you! Where is your walker? You don't have a cane or anything?" I said no. It was obvious that I was walking just fine, slowly, but no wobbling, but since she knew what I had been through, it did not make sense to her that I did not have something to assist me walking. But I did not need anything.

    My biggest challenge upon leaving the hospital was walking upstairs. My six therapy sessions did not start until two weeks after I was released, so I practiced walking up and down the stairs in the building, taking walks outside around the block and getting on the bus to go short distances around town. By the time the therapy started, I was far beyond the exercises they had for me. When the occupational therapist came, she stayed for 10 minutes because everything that she had planned to teach me to do such as getting in and out of the bed, showering, and navigating in the kitchen, I had already been doing. She told me that if she had known the tasks that I was able to do, she wouldn't have come. She proceeded to cancel the remaining sessions that had been scheduled. Three weeks after I went to Linda's apartment, I took the Amtrak home to Harpers Ferry for the weekend. It was so good to be home and I was able to walk up the twenty steps to my apartment and walk around town. I moved back for good in the next couple of weeks after I finished going to all of my post-hospital appointments. Linda drove me home and we walked to a familiar spot, Bolivar Heights that has an inclined path leading to the top. I arrived at the top of the hill, and gazed at the beautiful mountains before leading her back to my place through a wooded path. I was home!

> *"Sometimes, the best thing that can happen to us is when our plans don't work out."*

SHE SPOKE IN A DIFFERENT LANGUAGE

Hope had visited me in the ICU and sometimes drove a friend to see me so she would not have to take public transportation. A week after I left the hospital, she, and a friend were talking on the phone. Apparently, Hope asked how I was doing so my friend handed me the phone. Knowing it was Hope that was on the other end of the phone, I greeted her in French asking her how she was. Greeting each other in French is something Hope, and I have periodically done through the years as we both speak just a little of the language. It is interesting because once I heard Hope's voice, I recall automatically greeting her as I did without any forethought. My friend told me later that Hope said to her "You just don't understand! Charlma was able to speak in a foreign language! This is a miracle." Hope knew that at one point I was not able to talk at all and that I was being assessed for brain damage. Our very short conversation, just a few words really, was indeed significant to Hope.

"*God can bring about the unexpected.*

YOU WILL DANCE AGAIN; AND SO, IT WAS

As I lay in ICU on life support, non-responsive, dependent on dialysis, etc., it made sense for statements to be spoken such as "She may not make it" or "If she does make it, she will not be like before" or "She will need a trach." Some of the witnesses heard these statements, other witnesses made these statements, and others were told these statements from other witnesses. Based on the data and statistics of cases like mine, the statements were reasonable. However, there were some that despite seeing my tube dependent body believed and made different declarations! One such person was my friend Patrice, who told me that during one of her visits when I was in ICU, "Charlma, God said you will dance again." I was in a coma at that time so I did not hear those prophetic words.

Four months after I was released from the hospital, I texted a picture to Patrice of some shoes I wore to the Bat Mitzvah of a co-worker's daughter. The text message sent with the picture said: "Part of my testimony…I danced in these shoes all night on Saturday at a Bat Mitzvah celebration. To God be the Glory!!!" I explained further that each step I danced was a praise to God… a 'thank you

Lord' for restoring me beyond what anyone could have imagined. I recall consciously thanking God within as I danced. Little did I know at the time that I forwarded the picture that it was a confirmation for Patrice because she had not yet told me what she whispered in my ear when I was in ICU. The prophetic word spoken in my ear in the ICU had manifested indeed. God is truly amazing!

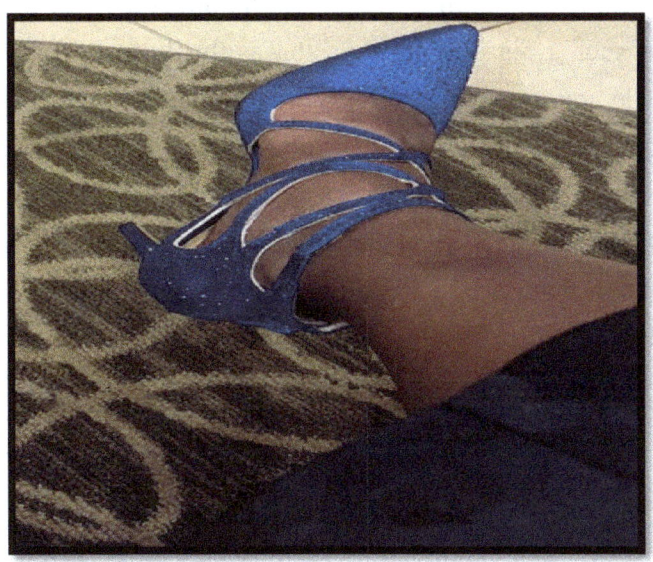

Praising God can occur anywhere; in this case, I was at a bat mitzvah!

YOU ARE A MIRACLE: DEAD BUT NOW ALIVE

It was early January 2019 when I had been dropped off by an Uber at the hospital where I had spent 6 weeks. I had arrived for my first post-release doctor's appointment, one of several that had been scheduled with various specialists. I walked down the hall, aware of each step I took and still amazed that I could walk easily with no assistance, not even a cane. Walking down the hall that day was such a big deal for me. It was thrilling and I rejoiced inside remembering how not too many weeks prior, someone would have had to wheel be in a bed down that same hallway. However, to the medical personnel, patients, visitors, and other people walking down the corridor that day, I was just another nameless person in the hallway. But I was not 'nameless' as my doctor would soon remind me.

"You…are…a…miracle!" One of the Resident's from the ICU said to me after I walked in her office and sat down. She continued "You were dead, and now you are alive!" and then proceeded to look at her computer screen to bring up information she wanted to discuss with me during my appointment. Those words had not been spoken to me so clearly as that up to that point. I had heard things like "you were really in bad shape," "Your heart stopped", "Your organs shut down" etc. But without speaking in technical medical terminology or flowery words, this doctor said very simply "You are a miracle!" You were dead and now you are alive!" The words hung in the air, and I am not positive I heard her next question or comment because I was shocked to be honest. I had not expected that. I thought she would be very impressed that I walked into the exam room on my own without needing even a cane or walker. Indeed, I was feeling happy about that. But she went much deeper than commenting on that! A few minutes later, her supervisor came into the room smiling and staring at me because he had been told my story by first-hand accounts, read my records, and was amazed at my state on that day. Looking at me and acknowledging what he had been told by the Resident he said, "you are a miracle." He then set his gaze toward the Resident and said, "she will remember you for the rest of her career!"

> *Sometimes the word "miracle" is the best description, even from a doctor!*

CLOTHED AND IN MY RIGHT MIND

"They came to Jesus and observed the man who had been demon-possessed sitting down, clothed and in his right mind..." Mark 5:15 (NAS)

When I heard my grandfather pray out loud, he frequently thanked God for being *"clothed and in his right mind"*. It wasn't until I was older that I recognized what a big deal it was to have a sound mind and 'right' thoughts. This language of being clothed and in one's right mind comes from an account in the New Testament found in the Gospels of Mark and Luke about a man possessed by devils and who lived in a tomb, naked cutting himself with stones. Jesus set this man free from the demons that had possessed his mind for so long. The Bible tells us that after the man's encounter with Jesus when people saw the man, he was "sitting at the feet of Jesus, clothed, and in his right mind..." Luke 8:35. Why do I mention this account you may ask? My story is different in that I was not demon possessed nor living in a state of isolation, but it is similar because as a result of Jesus intervening in my situation in the ICU, I am in my right mind despite what the science said should have been my reality.

Based on science, I should have diminished mental capacity. After having flat lined without a pulse for 26 minutes, it was reasonable that my mind would certainly be impacted...that I would have some degree of brain damage. A simple internet search will show that irreversible brain damage is likely after ten minutes without oxygen and my heart had stopped for over twice that amount of time. Yes, I had finally been resuscitated by the CPR team that refused to stop their efforts to revive me but regaining a pulse was only part of the battle. I was not out of the woods after being resuscitated. One article I read written by a physician in New York stated that "Research generally suggests that about 40 percent of patients who receive CPR after experiencing cardiac arrest in a hospital survive immediately after being resuscitated, and only 10 to 20 percent survive long enough to be discharged." [31] Further, even with the 10 to 20 percent that would survive to be discharged, there was still the likelihood that there would be impact to my brain. In one of the early family meetings at the hospital, my cousin Dari told me that the topic of the degree to which my brain might be impacted was discussed. Even without the brain damage, they predicted that I would have some diminished capacity; that

---

[31] The CPR We Don't See on TV, by Dhruv Khullar, M.D. July 17, 2014, 11:00.

my mental state would not be the same. Based on the facts surrounding my condition and medical expertise, it was the responsibility of the medical staff to inform my family and that is what they did. They prepared my family and friends for the likelihood that if I did survive, and come out of the coma, I would need an assisted living situation. But God had a different plan.

> *"The predictions of people do not always match the results that God brings forth."*

GOD MAKES ALL THINGS NEW

"And he that sat upon the throne said, Behold, I make all things new." Revelation 21:5

"Godmommy, God said He makes All things new!" I was quiet after hearing that statement; still holding the phone, but quiet. I was on the phone with one of my Goddaughters, Blue Diana. She continued talking because we had a lot to catch up on, but as she continued, I finally just said "Shhhhh...don't say anything else right now!" I did not want to be rude, but I just needed to savor those words and take hold of their power. I was sure they were prophetic words for me, "God makes all things new!"

In the month that I was released from the hospital, I did not talk on the phone much, not because I couldn't talk, it was just that I didn't want to. The volume of my voice was low as my throat healed from all of the tubes and I wanted to preserve my voice. Also, I was very particular about the things I wanted to talk about. I was still reflecting...still processing, the miracle that had occurred in my life and I preferred being quiet. It was a very introspective time for me. Typical everyday conversation was not anything I wanted to engage in. But, on this day during the first month of my release from the hospital, I was having a conversation with Blue Diana. It is always great to talk to her and at some point, in any of our conversations we will always end up talking about the goodness of Jesus and all He continues to do in our lives. So, at some point in the conversation, she said to me "God says He's making all things new!" It felt like those words had leaped within me if that were possible. I responded, "Amen!" Yes. Jesus makes all things new."

    The words "all things new" kept ringing in my ears and explained a lot about how I was feeling; new. They were confirmation of a message I had received from a co-worker when I was in the hospital. One of the teams that I work with sent me a gift box that included a smaller box with encouraging and inspirational messages from various people. One message was simple, but profound. It said that I was going to be stronger than I was before. Since leaving the hospital, I have experienced a keener awareness of God's love and greater peace. I have always loved people; people from all walks of life whether we had anything in common or not, but I felt an even greater love for people. Within months after being released from the hospital, I realized one day as I was out hiking that I felt physically strong which seemed strange to me because in January 2019, I was practicing walking a couple of miles a day and was still having difficulty going up and down the stairs because my body was recovering. But in a little over two weeks from that time, I was able to navigate the streets of DC by carefully walking to the bus stop to take the city bus and using the subway system. All this was prior to the physical therapist who had been set up to assist me showing up. By the end of the month, I told a friend that I had walked up one hundred stairs the previous day. I was surprised by the speed with which God was restoring me. At no time did I feel as though I was pushing myself. I was consistent with practicing going up and down the stairs because that was my greatest challenge upon leaving the hospital, but I was not straining or pushing myself. The words of my Goddaughter and co-worker were a preview of what was to come.

God's plan was not to just restore my mind and body back to where it was before the events that led me to ICU, but to do more. I say this because to restore means "to bring back to or put back into a former or original state."[32] At some point after I was released from the hospital, I realized that my mind was not back to its former or original state; it was better...so much better. I was amazed. My thoughts were clearer, my capacity for navigating between vastly different subject matters had increased, and the time it took me to analyze information was significantly shorter. I was better...so much better. I

[32] Merriam Webster

certainly could not have made my mind better nor could any doctor. There was no pill or process that did this. No, God made all things new.

> *God has made all things new.*

NINETY-NINE PERCENT MORTALITY

In the late summer/early fall of 2019, I sat around laughing with some high-school friends, two of whom I have known since kindergarten and first grade, for a short end-of-summer get away in Florida. We ate snacks, reminisced, and talked about life. In talking about life, our discussion turned to death which was inevitable because my two childhood friends Rosemary and Elaine were with me in the ICU. Elaine is a doctor and Rosemary a retired dentist and public health professional. Ninety-nine percent!" Elaine said passionately. I looked at her. "They didn't tell you that did they? Ninety-nine percent is the mortality rate of what happened to you, and you were in the 1% that survived!" Rosemary said, "yeah girl, you are patient "A". I'm surprised they haven't written a journal article about you." Elaine went on to say "I was in the ICU researching and looking up the possible things that could go wrong with your condition and I kept checking the boxes. Yup, that is going on, check; that's happening, check; this is happening too, check!" Everything that could potentially go wrong, was in fact happening.

I am so happy that Jesus is not subject to the percentages derived by the knowledge of people no matter how educated they are. Despite the 1% chance of surviving an illness. God always has the final say. No matter how things look; God has the final say.

> *"God always has the final say in your life."*

HOW WOULD I KNOW?

For those who did not know my testimony, there was no evidence of what I had been through. On this point, about 7 months after I left the hospital, I shared my testimony with someone in the town where I live who I see often. He looked at me quizzically after I told him what had happened and asked "Wow, when did this happen?" When I told him, he said "I didn't know…but how would I?" In other words, I didn't look like I had been through what I was describing. Many people said similar things to me at various times since my release. One friend sort of summed it up when four months after I was released and we were at an event together, she smiled at me when she first saw me said "That's just like God to make it so that you don't look like what you've been through!"

God is so merciful, and I am thankful!

> *"Sometimes God leaves no evidence of how you were Before his touch."*

HIS EXPECTATIONS WERE HIGHER

It was February 1, 2019, an icy, lightly snowy day and I was meeting Monet and Nellie for lunch. They are family though not through blood. Nellie's son Cole, a God given nephew, was also coming and I was super excited that he was joining us. I had been out of the hospital almost a month at this point and was looking forward to seeing them. I felt such a sense of freedom and gratitude doing familiar things like walking the streets of DC to meet at a restaurant since laying in a hospital bed everyday was not a distant memory. My Goddaughter Asia, Monet's daughter, had recently relocated from the DMV area when she was contacted about me being in the hospital. That call answered her question as to why she had not heard from me when I returned from traveling as I told her she would. Also, it let her know why I had not responded to her call to me and her voice message where she asked that I call her and her fiancé Terrance back because they had something to ask me. Under normal circumstances, there was no way that I would not have responded to a message like that. It was Asia who told her family about me being in the hospital.

The last time I had seen Monet and Nellie, I was in the hospital, not in the ICU but still in the hospital. By the time they had come to see me, I had really improved and doing well considering the state I had previously been in. During their visit I was feeding myself, yet I had not even been able to push the button on the nurse call remote when I first moved to the room. However, I would later learn that when Monet and Nellie visited me, they were alarmed at what they saw. I remember telling them that I was sleepy, but none of what was before them registered because, again, they had not seen me in the ICU and did not know the details of what had gone on. Nellie came to visit me again a couple of weeks later with her husband Binky and I was much more alert during that visit and at that point had started walking down the hall with the aid of a walker and a nurse.

We sat at the table talking, laughing as we always do at some point, and deciding what we were going to order. At one point, Nellie said "When we told Cole about you being in the hospital, he said "Aunt Charlma will be climbing up that mountain again in a few months!"" He was referring to a challenging trail in Harpers Ferry, Maryland Heights, one of the most popular ones that he,

Asia and her husband Terrance, his brother Kyle, and Asia's brother Aaron and more of their family had joined me on years earlier. As I turned to Cole, he smiled, nodding his head yes. Although at that time I was about 30 to 35 pounds under my typical weight, he did not seem phased by that and did not back down from his prediction. He appeared to have unwavering confidence. I thought to myself, "He has no idea what I have been through. Does he know that I almost died; that my heart had stopped over 20 minutes?" Honestly, being able to hike that trail was not something I was even praying about at that point. I was more than content with the life I had been granted whether it included that or not. One thing was for sure, Cole's expectations were higher than mine!

Four months after that lunch I decided to climb Maryland Heights. I was able to do it with ease and as I ascended, I periodically stopped and said, "Thank You Jesus!" "Lord, I thank You!" I even lifted my hands and pranced at points. At some time during my upward climb, it dawned on me that I needed to call Cole. I needed to let him know that his prophetic words had come to pass! The reception was not good enough for me to make a call, but I was able to post on Facebook a few pictures of me on the trail and text a message to Cole. I sent him a text saying,

"Look at my Facebook post sweetie!" His response was "You made it!" Yes, I had made it. To God Be the Glory!

Cole and I at the Restaurant outing in early February 2019

NO BROKEN BONES; NOT ONE

In the months and years following me leaving the hospital, events continue to occur that put into perspective what God did for me. Without question, I will be profoundly impacted for the rest of my life. It does not have to be a major event that reminds me of what God has done. It is typically just a routine event like a conversation with a friend or someone I'm meeting for the first time. It might be a photograph, the smell of disinfectant, or the sound of a beeping machine or a food served while I was in the hospital and I'll reflect on how incredibly merciful God is. I call these trigger events. In my workplace there are always trigger events, but I'll share one.

I stood in the doorway of a colleague's office and started our conversation in a typical manner asking how he was and what he had done over the weekend. The conversation began to take a turn for me as he started to describe that his brother-in law was ill, and that CPR was performed for about 5 minutes and that he had some fractured bones in his chest due to the CPR and was recovering. I recall standing there, motionless when he made that comment. He went on to say that someone else in his family who is a Resident said about his brother-in-law's broken bones, "of course he had fractured bones after undergoing CPR for that amount of time." When he said that, I was stunned. In that short amount of time, my mind flashed back to my situation. I reminded my colleague that CPR had been performed on me for 26 minutes (perhaps, he really didn't know that detail). I went on to tell him that I did not have any broken bones. He looked at me and said, "no broken bones?!" I responded "No." It is moments like this that can be a bit surreal for me. Moments in everyday life that trigger memories of miracles...of the extraordinary. My mind quickly went back to a conversation with my childhood friend Elaine, an amazing doctor who was in the ER with me when I coded. During one of her visits to my regular hospital room as she was reflecting on the CPR, she said, "We just knew you would have broken bones in your chest!" She went on to explain that the technician performing the CPR, known to be the best, was a really huge guy. One person told me he was about 6 ft 3 inches or more and looked to be about 230 pounds. He is said to have pounded on my small chest with what looked like all his might for 26 minutes. Let that sink in...26 minutes with full force!

After doing a little research, I found that it is generally reported that 30% of people receiving CPR experience fractures to ribs. If you add to that general percentage the specific fact that I am a woman with a small to medium frame being pounded on by a very large man, for such a long time, I'd imagine that percentage would increase. In one study, data from over two-thousand patients was analyzed and it was found that there were skeletal chest injuries in 91% of women and rib fractures in 85% of women. [33] Again, although medical statistics and probabilities would say that several of my bones, some bones, or at least one bone would be broken, that did not occur. God can change any situation, at any time, in any way, for anybody. No broken bones. No, not one!

---

[33] *What Happens if Ribs break during CPR?, March 7, 2018, | Dr. Mary Williams, RN, DC.*

CIRCLING BACK

Return home and tell how much God has done for you. So the man went away and told all over town how much Jesus had done for him. Luke 8:39

I call it "circling back": returning home or to other familiar places and telling people how much God has done for me! Sometimes, the "telling" hasn't been verbal...it was just showing up so people who saw me when I was in the hospital or heard about me could see for themselves what God had done. I never made some grand pronouncement saying "look at me" because that was not necessary. Instead, the opportunities to circle back occurred during everyday events such as sitting in a coffee shop talking to a neighbor, I hadn't seen in almost a year who had heard something about my situation though not the details and telling me that she had chills as I talked filling in the blanks of the story she had heard. Or, it was going for a hike with a girlfriend who I used to work with who saw me when I was in a coma and who came to visit me in Harpers Ferry; walking into my office building about a month and a half after being released from the hospital and talking to a few people who were aware of my ordeal and watching one colleague look at me and shake his head, in disbelief, given how I was at that moment compared to how he heard I had been or it could simply be chatting with friends online. I had the opportunity to see my sister-friend Darla and her husband Wayne when I was in San Francisco on a work trip after returning to work. We met near the famous Pier 39 and had dinner with the biggest smiles on our faces the whole time. Darla and Wayne had been some of those who had fervently prayed for me.

When some people heard second hand about what had gone on with me, but hadn't seen me lying in the bed in ICU looking as though I was on the brink of death on my worst days, when they saw me a few months later they thought that perhaps my condition had not been as bad as they had heard because if it had been, I wouldn't be in the condition that I was in, in such a short time frame. One such person told me two months after I had been released from the hospital and had returned to work that I didn't look as though anything had been wrong. He said he had not heard the details of what my situation had been, but that I looked normal. During encounters like that, If I started explaining things like I had no pulse for 26 minutes or that I was in a coma for a few weeks or that I had to learn to walk again, I would be met with expressions that told me they were trying to match the words they heard with what they were seeing. It is so powerful to go to places to visit people who actually saw me during the worst days of my ICU stay, and then they see me...experience me. My presence and everything that it entailed spoke for itself. Words were not necessary. When I 'circled back' and went to my office in the middle of February to let my manager know that I planned to return to work in a couple of weeks, one of the people he took me to see was a senior manager, a medical doctor with an extensive background in the area of Neurology. When we walked in the office and greeted each other, the doctor at one point glanced out the window for a bit before turning to me and saying, "I can honestly say, in all my years of practicing medicine, that I've never seen anyone go through what you've been through who could walk in here, talking, with a cup of coffee in their hand as though it's nothing!" Comments like this continued to bring home for me what a mighty, mighty work the Lord had performed! Truly, God had performed a miracle.

During these circling back trips, my presence and everything it represented was a declaration, loud and clear,

> *"It is important to share what god has done in your life and the lives of others."*

that not only had God spared my life but that He had strengthened and restored me beyond what anyone could have imagined. During a 9 - month period before the one-year mark of me going to the ICU, I travelled taking planes, trains, buses, or cars to about fifteen places for work, vacation, relaxation, visits with family and friends and other purpose driven trips. I never set out to go to X number of places to testify of God's goodness, but I took advantage of the opportunities presented. Each trip allowed me to show up and declare the great things God had done and continued to do in my life. Just like the scripture cited above where Jesus told the man who he had healed, to go home and tell the great things that God has done, we too need to take the time to go, to circle back, and tell people what God has done!

WAITING FOR THE OTHER SHOE TO DROP

Many people in this country have heard the expression "waiting for the other shoe to drop." For those who have not heard this idiomatic phrase, it means to wait for an expected and inevitable event to occur. The event is most often negative. When this idiom is used, it is after some event has occurred and another event is expected to inevitably follow."[34] This phrase relates to my situation because from the time I was released from the hospital and even up to this day, there are some people who have been 'waiting for the other shoe to drop'! Not because anyone wants me to be sick again; of course not. It is just that it would be natural given how critical my situation was, for a relapse to occur or that I would be more susceptible to illnesses. But that has not been my situation. I can always tell by the expectant look or tone in their voices when they ask me how I am doing now as though they are bracing themselves for me to tell them something bad. How could I be ok...for real?!

[34] www.idioms.online.

Yes, they heard me when I told them about the miracle that God had performed in healing and restoring me, but it was like I could sense them thinking "yeah, yeah… but how are you?" "How are you really doing?" "What are the special accommodations you need?" When I would respond that I felt stronger and better than I had before…some would give me blank stares. Even if I would have had diminished capacity or was not quite back to what had previously been 'normal', I would have still been abundantly grateful for God's mercy in sparing my life. However, God is the author of my story, and it did not include diminished capacity or recurring sicknesses.

IT HAPPENS AT SOME OF THE CRAZIEST TIMES!

"I will bless the Lord at all times: his praise shall be continually in my mouth." Psalm 34:1

It happens at some of the craziest times; while carrying six bags of groceries because the four items I intended to buy when I went into the store somehow turned into thirty items by the time I reached the checkout register. Or, while walking up the escalator steps at a metro station in Washington, DC., either by choice or because there is a mechanical problem making it necessary. At times like these the stark reality of my current life hits me. The reality that the same person who at one point was too weak to even push the little button on the remote control used to call the nurses for help or who celebrated when she was able to take 3 feeble steps with the aid of a walker to get from the bed to the bedside commode is now walking up stairs and carrying multiple bags at once! And, when the reality hits me words of praise…the blessings to the Lord automatically flow from my mouth: "Thank You Jesus!" …." You are merciful God!" …. "Thank You Lord!" …or simply "Wow God!" Sometimes the praises come unexpectedly in the middle of me doing something that most people would describe as 'routine.' I do not try to hold back my expressions. One such time that comes to mind was two months after I left the hospital and had already returned to work. I was in my office working on a project. I was using two computer monitors, cutting information from one screen, and pasting it to the second screen where I was drafting a document, and then referencing a hard copy document that I had on my desk. I was proceeding with the ease that one would expect from someone in my position, but not from someone who had been in a coma 3 or 4 months earlier, whose loved ones had been told would likely have some brain damage and who after leaving ICU to go to a step-down room, was asked every day whether she knew what day it was, where she was, or who the president was! So, while seamlessly carrying out this routine, I thought "Wow, this may look normal, but it's not normal at all!" The reality of my situation overtook me like a tsunami wave! The memory of where I had been and where God brought me from so very quickly was profound. At that moment, tears of gratitude started to flow, and the praises started to come out of my mouth! No, I was not inside a church building singing songs from a hymnal or words on a screen. I was at work, in my office, and at that moment, it was the most appropriate place in the world to let God know how very thankful I was! I will bless the Lord at all times, and I will allow His praises to flow from my mouth!

The message here is not that it took the events that occurred in the latter part of 2018 and early 2019 for me to appreciate everyday things and praise God for them, because I have always been very thankful for small things (a pretty rock, a sunny day, the ability to have a good meal) and I am well aware of the source of all the blessings in my life. But I am keenly aware that everyday tasks should also be celebrated and not taken for granted. They are also part of my miracle because, but for the intervention of Jesus in that ICU and beyond, I wouldn't be doing them at all; they would not be possible.

> *"There are everyday things all around to be thankful for."*

> "For my thoughts are not your thoughts, neither are your ways my ways', declares the Lord. As the heavens are higher than the earth, so are my ways higher than your ways and my thoughts than your thoughts." Isaiah 55:8-9.

POWER IN THE PROCESS

Why? Why did all of this happen in the first place and why was in not stopped? These are questions many may ask whether they say it aloud or just within. Some might ask whether what I went through could have been prevented? Why didn't God just heal in an instant? Why didn't God just prevent my heart from stopping and all of the circumstances that followed that event? Certainly, in the blink of an eye, God could have brought me from sickness to health, but there is Power in the Process. Others may ask why God even needed to intervene in the first place. What was my part in all of this? If things had been done differently at various points leading up to November 21, 2018, such as if I had not taken the trip to Wales, maybe a miracle would not have been necessary; maybe there would have been no need for divine intervention. Maybe that is true…maybe, but not necessarily.

None of the doctors attributed my situation to any one thing nor were they able to identify a singular cause, one doctor compared my situation to "a perfect storm," a combination of several factors working together while another told me that they don't know what happened. If one thing, or a couple of things had been different perhaps

November 21st would have been different. But we could indeed say that about many events, circumstances and experiences that take place during our lifetimes; if just one thing were different or if I had made a different choice, a particular outcome would be different. However, my testimony is not just about the outcome. The trials I went through presented practical opportunities for God to reveal himself to me and everyone that was in any way connected.

If we focus just on the resolution of challenging situations, we might miss the fruit yielded in the in-between period; we miss the power of the process. It is in the in-between stage that transformation takes place. As a result of my story, there are people; witnesses who have talked about having a greater level of faith. There are medical personnel who now know that scientific wisdom is not the supreme deciding factor as to what will happen to a chronically ill patient and that even when they have determined they can do nothing else for a patient, that determination is not necessarily the end of the story. There are those who did not believe in God, who said they now do. Even if there are those who still do not believe in God and the miraculous, at a minimum, this experience should cause them to question, re-evaluate, or ponder their beliefs. There is power in the process.

> "Transformation takes place during the 'in between' stage."

Section VIII

Second Breath of Life Hike; Celebrating Anniversaries

SECOND BREATH OF LIFE HIKE

Cultures around the world celebrate or otherwise acknowledge important events and milestones. Some celebrate expectant mothers, birthdays, a good harvest, wedding anniversaries, advancements in school or the 'coming of age' of children to adulthood. Some acknowledgements aren't joyous but are still needed like Memorial Day in the United States where men and women who died while serving in the U.S. Military are honored. For me, having a special celebration commemorating what God had done for me during this miraculous season of my life was something I was excited to do. It was not to be taken for granted. The first thing was to decide when, that is what date, would be set aside. The first date that came to mind was November 21, 2018, when I entered the ICU, my heart stopped for 26 minutes, and I was revived. I also thought about the day the medical staff told my family that there was nothing else they could do, I wasn't responding in the way they thought I should and that they recommended removing me from life support. The thing that caused me to shy away from memorializing those conversations is that it was not just one conversation like that. Also, while some of the witnesses were either engaged in conversations like that or heard them, it was unlikely that they would remember the exact date. But then, January 4th was really significant as the culmination of all my previous days and when I was released from the hospital. Although I celebrate life and my blessings every day, I was positive that I wanted to mark a specific day to honor God and I ended up choosing November 21st, because that was like no other day for me!

On the first-year anniversary, November 21, 2019, I hiked a trail I had never done before but had always been curious about. It was steeper and about two miles longer than the trail to the Maryland Heights overlook, my favorite trail.[35] I felt great hiking this unfamiliar path alone, praying and thanking God for His mercy; in awe with each step. I was amazed that it was not a struggle like I would have expected it to be even if I had not gone through what I had. It was though I had been recalibrated or something. As I hiked the path that was a continuous uphill journey, I reflected on how less than a year earlier, I had to learn to walk again and had been excited when I took just three steps with a walker. Wow God… just Wow! It was a wonderful celebration.

---

[35] Maryland Heights is a popular hiking trail in Harpers Ferry, WV.

As my 2020 anniversary date approached, I asked myself how I would celebrate. I could always hike Maryland Heights. As I pondered that point, I had a flashback to when I was in my hospital room and the staff was assisting my family and I looked for an appropriate physical and occupational therapy location for when I left the hospital. The therapists wanted to get me to a point where I could stand up by myself, walk with a walker, and do minimal tasks such as going to the bathroom by myself. I told the doctor that I wanted a therapy location that would help me get to a point where I would be strong enough to walk around my town of Harpers Ferry and the streets of DC, and one day even hike again. I remember the sympathetic look one doctor had as though she thought it was unlikely that I would ever get to that point. But, because she had such a wonderful bedside manner, she said "we will look for a place that will help you get stronger." I'll always remember her kindness.

I decided to invite some friends in the Washington, DC/Maryland/Virginia area to join me on the hike. I could not invite a lot of people and definitely not those out of town because the world was in the middle of the COVID-19 pandemic, and I would need to have protocols in place as advised by the governing bodies. Most of the people had seen me when I was in ICU and/or the hospital and had prayed for my recovery. They were witnesses and I thought it would be a wonderful experience to celebrate God's goodness together. I called the hike the "Second Breath of Life Hike." I got the name from my friend Pastor Larry Robbins who, after hearing my testimony about how God raised me up said "that sounds like a second breath of life to me…"

It was a wonderful celebration and there were eighteen of us who participated that day including two local friends that along with me each led a smaller segment of the larger group, so that we could be properly spaced apart and paced. We were challenged and reflected on why we were doing the hike. One thing that I told everyone before we started the hike was that it was important that we not forget what the Lord has done and what they witnessed then and now! A couple of people who participated in the hike chronicled the day through posts on social media:

<u>"SECOND BREATH OF LIFE HIKE"</u>

What an Awesome Day with a Miracle Walking in the Flesh!...

This Woman of God Not Only Defied The Claws of Death but Defied "Every" Limitation and Expectation of the Medical System pressing to Return to the Top of "This" Mountain Multiple Times!

Her Story is AMAZING & So is this Hike to The Top of This Mountain Overlooking Harpers Ferry in West Virginia!!!...

What a day!
Hiking for the first time in Harper's Ferry with our Friend and Sister in Lord. Celebrating her "Second Breath"! I will not tell her story as it is her's to tell! Frank and I are just thankful to be a part of the story. And, to witness the Power and Love of God over His daughter!!

One year ago, God allowed me to witness and participate in a miracle. Charlma Quarles. To God be the Glory! Still in awe of God!

"Remembering past blessings of God, strengthens us in this journey of life."

THE MIRACLE, THE WITNESSES AND ME

THE MIRACLE, THE WITNESSES AND ME

THE MIRACLE, THE WITNESSES AND ME

THE MIRACLE, THE WITNESSES AND ME

NOT ROUTINE

It was a very cold morning in the winter of 2022, and I stood on the platform of the train station in Harpers Ferry, WV waiting for the commuter train that would take me into Washington, DC for work. At one point, as the cold wind blew across my face and I heard the train steadily approaching, I closed my eyes, smiled and tilted my head back a little to savor the moment, I was profoundly aware in that moment that it was a privilege to be able to enjoy what I was experiencing. I was standing independently, feeling the cold air, hearing the train, and on my way to work. I quietly said "Wow, thank you God!" On this morning, I realized yet again that the most routine experiences will never really be "routine" to me and that they will always provide me with an opportunity to lift up praises!

JESUS IS A HEALER...STILL

Jesus is a healer, and he still heals today.
Not everyone gets healed, but
Jesus is still a healer.
My mother died, my friend died, your
Brother died, her sister's child died...we prayed,
They died, but nonetheless, Jesus is a healer.

The bible says "this sickness is not unto death, but that
God will be glorified." God will be glorified.
god is glorified. Look around.
The earth is full of the glory of God!

Only God knows the day or the hour...no man knows.
We pray and some survive, we pray and some die, but
People are to always pray and not grow weary.
Jesus is a healer.

Who will live? Who will die? We don't know, so
What should we do?
We should pray...always pray...always.
They say it doesn't look good, but...
Jesus is a healer.

THE MIRACLE, THE WITNESSES AND ME

Some say I died, but then I survived!
Either way, God is in control and wants us to pray.

It looked bad...really bad...don't expect much they said.
I was restored, above and beyond.
Was I lucky? No! Jesus is a healer.
Still!

BOOK REVIEW

BY PHILLIPA L. ANDERSON

The author's authentic voice takes you on her journey from death to life to living. The reader becomes a witness. The reader-witness becomes a believer that there is more to living through life's journey than what we feel or touch. The 'reader-witness' begins to believe there is a force within us and larger than us. That force brings life, peace, and hope.

On a personal note – I have been working through my parent's passing only four months apart. I had been going through the process of selling their home, probate and all of death's aftermath. It took me a while to begin the draft after receiving it. When I finally did, I could not put it down. I experienced peace.; It was a balm. If there's a yearning for evidence of the substance of things not seen, please read this book.

Phillipa L. Anderson,

Friend

Washington, DC

BOOK REVIEW

BY DARI MALLOY

The forward opens with a summary of events that inspired the author to embark on a journey sharing her testimony, a testimony many may relate to, a story that "is our story." It encourages the reader to reflect on what we celebrate and commemorate, why we celebrate it, and how we share that experience with others. A realization that the power of prayer and God's mercy is present in every step that we take. One gains insight into the significance of memorializing the beginning of that "Second Breath of Life...". It invites the reader to uncover more details about the miracle witnessed.

Dari Malloy, MA,

Cultural Anthropologist
Bronx, NY

BOOK REVIEW

BY LYNN PECHUEKONIS

If you are a believer in miracles, you will love Charlma's inspiring testimony about her journey back from the brink of death. You'll absolutely wish you could have been part of that crowd of witnesses who prayed over her and watched the amazing transition from life support to living proof of God's intervention. If you are a miracle skeptic, Charlma is authentic and gracious enough to allow your questions yet engage you thoroughly in her fascinating story of faith, fellowship, and extraordinary healing.

Lynn Pechuekonis

Author of *The Gentle Savior: Seeing Jesus Through the Eyes of the Women Who Met Him*
Harpers Ferry, WV

ABOUT THE AUTHOR

Elder Charlma Quarles is an ordained minister who has a burden for the people of God to be empowered and living in accordance with God's design in Scripture and for those who do not yet know Jesus or who have rejected Him. God has granted her the opportunity to minister in the United States, Asia and Africa in local churches, conferences, discipleship training, and assisting with church plants in hard-to-reach areas. During the COVID-19 pandemic, minister Charlma started a grass roots movement called 'Share Your Plate' to reach some people in nations with severe lockdown restrictions and other impacts due to COVID-19. Since April 2020, as a result of this ministry, thousands of people in India, Kenya, the Navajo Nation, and the Philippines have received food, been prayed for, and told about Jesus Christ with salvations following by the 'Share Your Plate' ministry partners in the nations served. Other projects such provision of bibles, housing, building a church/school building and starting a community, collaborative garden for women in Eastern Kenya to care for have also resulted from this ministry.

Although she has not given birth to any children, she has been blessed to be a 'mom', godmother, auntie mentor and spiritual mother to a host of children, teenagers, and young adults.

Contact her at: charqua123 gmail.com

www.ingramcontent.com/pod-product-compliance
Lightning Source LLC
Chambersburg PA
CBHW070951180426
43194CB00042B/2214